HEBREW GRAMMAR

FOR BEGINNERS

WM. B. STEVENSON, B.D.

Bala Theological College

WIPF & STOCK • Eugene, Oregon

Wipf and Stock Publishers
199 W 8th Ave, Suite 3
Eugene, OR 97401

Hebrew Grammar for Beginners
By Stevenson, William B.
ISBN 13: 978-1-60608-101-3
Publication date 7/22/2008
Previously published by George Adam Young & Co., 1904

PREFACE

Part I. of the following pages supplies a first year's course in Hebrew Grammar, and is based on the writer's lecture notes. The attempt has been made to combine concentration upon essentials with a certain fulness in the form of the exposition. Additional particulars, chiefly for reference, are given in smaller type. Possibly the grammar may be of use to those who cannot obtain the help of a teacher. The vocabularies are intended to be thoroughly mastered. The allusions to Welsh forms and idioms are a special feature.

After the completion of Part I., private students are recommended to learn the verbs in Table 12, with some assistance from the explanations given in Part II. It will then be possible for them without much difficulty to read the first chapter of the book of Ruth. Part II. contains full notes on the Hebrew verb, and is designed to be part of a second year's course.

Particular attention is requested to the Additional Note on next page.

WM. B. STEVENSON.

BALA, *September*, 1904.

ADDITIONAL NOTE.

As exceptions to the rule that the Hebrew accent falls on the last syllable, it should be observed that (*a*) the verbal terminations named in § 2, (*b*) the ending נִי of the personal pronouns (§§ 6, 7), and (*c*) the endings of the Hebrew words for "these" and "those" (§ 8) are all unaccented.

ERRATA.

In § 46 note *c*, for Table 12 read Table 14.

In § 47 note *b*, for Table 12 read Table 14.

CONTENTS

PART I.

PART II.

PART I.

ELEMENTS OF HEBREW GRAMMAR.

§ 1. HEBREW WRITING.*

Consonants.

Sign.			Name.	Trans-literation.
		א	’âleph	’
	ב	בּ	bêth	*b*, *bh*
	ג	גּ	gîmel	*g*, *gh*
	ד	דּ	dâleth	*d*, *dh*
		ה	hê	*h*
		ו	wâw	*w*
		ז	zayin	*z*
		ח	ḥêth	*ḫ* (*ch*), *ḥ*
		ט	ṭêth	*ṭ*
		י	yôdh	*y*
ך	כ	כּ	kaph	*k*, *kh*
		ל	lâmedh	*l*
	ם	מ	mêm	*m*
	ן	נ	nûn	*n*
		ס	sâmekh	*s*
		ע	‘ayin	‘, *ġ*
ף	פ	פּ	pê	*p*, *ph*
	ץ	צ	ṣâdhê	*ṣ*
		ק	ḳôph	*ḳ*
		ר	rêsh	*r*
	שׂ	שׁ	shîn, śîn	*sh*, *ś*
	ת	תּ	tâw	*t*, *th*

Vowels.

Sign.	Name.	Trans-literation.
◌ָ, ◌ָא, ◌ָה	ḳâmeṣ	*â*, *ŏ*
◌ַ	pathaḥ	*ă*
◌ֵ, ◌ֵי, ◌ֵא, ◌ֵה	ṣêrê	*ē*
◌ֶ, ◌ֶה	s‘ghôl	*ĕ*
◌ִ, ◌ִי	ḥîreḳ	*î*, *ĭ*
◌ֹ, וֹ	ḥôlem	*ô*
◌ֻ, וּ	ḳibbûṣ, shûreḳ	*û*, *ŭ*
◌ְ	sh‘wâ	$^{\cdot}$
◌ֲ	ḫâṭêph pathaḥ	^{a}
◌ֱ	ḫâṭêph s‘ghôl	^{e}
◌ֳ	ḫâṭêph ḳâmeṣ	^{o}

* The vowels in this table are to be pronounced as in Latin.

Introductory.—At first the Hebrew alphabet consisted of consonants only; none of the vowel-sounds were represented in writing. The vowel-signs now in use were invented several centuries after the Christian era. Their peculiar appearance and position are accounted for by their being an addition to the original system of writing. Because they are of late date and subordinate in character, it is often incorrectly said that the Hebrew alphabet consists of consonants only. The usually printed system of vowel-representation is not the only one; and there is also an older consonantal alphabet, which went out of use before the Christian era. The general direction of the writing is from right to left, and this should be remembered in writing each letter. ך, ם, ן, ף, ץ are special final forms to be used at the end of words. The forms of the printed consonants may be simplified somewhat in writing.

The pronunciation of a language cannot be satisfactorily learned by a beginner from a book; but the following remarks supply some general guidance on the subject. The pronunciation of the Massorites, who were the inventors of the vowel-signs, is usually followed by modern scholars. It is, of course, only the pronunciation of a particular period, chosen because we happen to know more about it than we do of other periods. Very little can be said about the pronunciation of the Biblical writers themselves, and even our knowledge of the Massorite pronunciation is imperfect. To modern Jews Hebrew is almost a foreign language, and their pronunciation has been influenced by the European languages they speak.

Duplicate Consonants.—It will be observed that there are three *s* signs, two *t*'s and two *k*'s. It is possible in the case of most consonants to pronounce them in a variety of distinctly different ways, and the *t*'s, *d*'s, *k*'s, *s*'s, *l*'s, &c. of different languages are by no means identical with one another. Even in the same language they may be pronounced differently by different individuals or in different words. The peculiarity of Hebrew, and of some other languages, is that it can distinguish some of these different pronunciations in writing.

NOTE.—It may be supposed that ג, ת, ס represent interdental sounds, while ק, ט, צ are pronounced emphatically and with the tongue raised higher up to the roof of the mouth. It is not certain that שׂ is different from ס, it may simply represent a ס which was originally שׁ.

Mutable Consonants.—The six stop consonants *p, t, k, b, d, g* mutate, as they do in Welsh. Each of them when mutated becomes the corresponding spirant; *e.g.*, *p* becomes *f*, *t* becomes *th* (in breath), *b* becomes *v*, *d* becomes Welsh *dd* (*th* in breathe). There is only one rule for mutation, with few exceptions: mutable consonants mutate when a vowel-sound precedes. The two sounds given to each of these six letters are distinguished in writing by the presence or absence of a dot in the bosom of the letters: פּ=p, פ=f, תּ=t, ת=th, &c.

NOTE.—The spirant sounds, as in Welsh, are to be regarded as later than the (original) stop sounds. So it need not surprise us to find traces of the old stop pronunciation after vowel-sounds, even in Massorite times; בָּתִּים and שְׁתַּיִ may be regarded as instances. כ had a sound like *ch* in German *ich*; the stream of breath strikes the front of the palate. When ח has the sound *ch* (*i.e.* *ḫ*), it is pronounced as in Welsh; the breath strikes the back of the palate. ג was perhaps pronounced like English *y* (compare English 'yield' from O.E. *gildan*; Welsh *gildio*). ג and ד are never mutated by modern Jews; the Sephardim do not even mutate ב and ת.

Glottal Consonants.—א is the glottal stop, the *coup de glotte*, or shock of the glottis, known to singers. It was very apt to become silent in Hebrew words. ע is not found in European languages. It had two sounds, as in other Semitic languages.

Other Consonants.—ח had two sounds also. It may be pronounced as Welsh *ch*. Its other sound, *ḥ*, was an emphatic *h* not found in English or Welsh. The remaining consonants may be pronounced as the English consonants opposite to them in the table. It should not be forgotten, however, that the pronunciation which is usual for these in our own language may not have been exactly that usual in Hebrew.

NOTE.—For example, *l* was no doubt pronounced as in French or Welsh, and not as in English; *r* seems to have been sometimes lingual and sometimes uvular.

The Position of the Vowels.—The Massorite vowels are not written alongside of the consonants. They are generally placed below that consonant which they follow in pronunciation; *ḥolem*, however, stands above the consonant which it follows. The vowels, accordingly, are to be read after the consonants below or above which they stand. There is one exception: *pathaḥ* following the last consonant of certain words is pronounced *before* that consonant, *e.g.* כֹּחַ (see § 4).

NOTE.—שׁ is to be read *shó* at the beginning of a word or syllable, but *óś* at the end. *Śó* is represented simply by שׂ and *ósh* by שׁ.

Vowel Pronunciation.—*Ḳameṣ* was pronounced by the Massorites *å* (long or short, similar to the vowels in English 'small' and 'hot'). But long ָ at an earlier period was *â* (in psalm), and most scholars give it this value. The rules given for distinguishing the cases where ָ is *â* and where *ŏ* are not much help to a beginner. The short value, *ŏ*, is infrequent. *Pathaḥ* is a very short *a*, more like that in English 'man' than in Welsh 'man,' and almost like *e* in 'men.' *Ṣere* is a very diphthongal *êⁱ* (like *a* in 'rate'). *S'ghol* is (short) *ĕ*. *Ḥireḳ* is long and short; the latter more Welsh than English. *Ḥolem* is a diphthongal *ôᵘ* (as in English 'wrote'). *Ḳibbuṣ* is long and short *u*, the Welsh vowel *w* (as in English 'moon' or 'true'). When written וּ it is called *shureḳ*.*

---

* For reading practice, see Vocabulary 1, which should now be learned.

Combined Representation of Vowels.—The simple vowel-signs are frequently joined to some one of the four consonants א, ו, י and ה, and the resulting combinations, given in the Table of Vowels, also represent the various vowel-sounds. Before the simple vowel-signs came into use these four consonants were used in a measure to represent the vowel-sounds. There was a pre-Massorite representation of vowels, in which ו signified *o* and *u*, י signified *i* and *e*, א represented chiefly *â*, and ה a variety of final vowels. When the new vowel-signs were invented, they were joined to the old signs so far as they existed. The combined representation so originating is frequently called complete, and the single representation defective; but the phraseology is bad, for there is nothing imperfect or incomplete about the single representation. ה at the end of words is so frequently used in combination with the Massorite vowels as a mere vowel-sign, that when it retains its consonantal value in this position it is written הּ. (This method of marking the consonantal value of ה at the end of words is sometimes extended to א, ו and י also.) The dot is called *mappîḳ*.

Note.—The consonants א, ו, י and ה first acquired a vocalic value in words where they ceased to be pronounced (as consonants). As the adjacent vowels were then generally long, these consonants came to represent principally long vowels. Accordingly, where the combined representation occurs it may generally be inferred that the vowel is long, but the simple representation stands equally for long or for short vowel-sounds.

Sh·was.—These are vowel-signs also, representing hurriedly pronounced vowel-sounds. The use of special letters to denote hurriedly pronounced vowels is proof of the minuteness with which the Massorites endeavoured to represent Hebrew speech in writing. *Simple vocal sh·wa* ְ is the most variable of the group; its exact pronunciation depends on the longer vowel which it replaces. It may be pronounced, for the sake of distinction, as *i* in English 'pin' (or as *u* in Welsh *pump*). *Ḥaṭeph pathaḥ*, as the name and the sign indicate, is a hurriedly pronounced *pathaḥ*, *ḥaṭeph s·ghol* a hurriedly pronounced *s·ghol*.

and *ḥaṭeph kameṣ* a hurried *ḳameṣ*. Because of their written form these are called compound *sh'was*. Syllables in which the vowel is *sh'wa* are not reckoned full syllables by the grammarians.

Silent Sh'wa.—The sign ְ has unfortunately another use than that just described. It often simply marks the end of a syllable. It must be written under every consonant that ends a syllable which is not final.* This *sh'wa* is called *sh'wa* silent to distinguish it from *sh'wa* vocal. The beginner cannot be given full rules to enable him to determine when ְ is vocal and when silent. The most useful points to observe are these: (1) when it follows the first consonant of a word it is vocal, *e.g.* בְּאֵר; also (2) when it precedes a mutated consonant, *e.g.* גְּדִי; also (3) when it is the second of two *sh'was* following successive consonants (the first being silent), *e.g.* יִקְטְלוּ.

Dâghêsh. — *Daghesh* is the dot which marks the stop pronunciation of the mutable letters, בּ is *b* while ב is *v*. When so used it is called *daghesh lene*, or light *daghesh*. It has, however, another use, namely to show that a consonant in which it is placed is doubled. Instead of a consonant being written twice over, it is written once and *daghesh* is inserted. This *daghesh* is *daghesh forte*, strong *daghesh*. Mutable consonants, when they are doubled, always keep their original stop value. Thus a mutable consonant, if it be doubled, does not mutate after a vowel.

Reading Exercise.

מִשְׁפָּט, גְּדִי, כָּתְבוּ, בְּאֵר, גַּנָּב, כֹּתְבִים, יִכְתֹּב, נִשְׁפְּטוּ, אֱלֹהִים,
הַבָּשָׂר, דִּבֵּר, דִּבֶּר, מְשֻׁלָּם, שִׁפֵּט, הִבְדִּיל, יִרְפֹּשׂ׃

Read and learn the nouns in Vocabulary 2.

---

* It is generally added, as an exception to this rule, that if a final syllable ends in two consonants, silent *sh'wa* is written under each; *e.g.* קֹשְׁטְ. Perhaps the second was originally vocal. Forms of this kind are few.

§ 2. THE ARTICLE.

In Hebrew, as in Welsh, indefinite nouns are used without a qualifying article. מֶלֶךְ is "a king." (See, however, § 39.)

The Definite Article has many forms. Originally it may have been *hal*. But the final consonant varies according to the initial consonant of the word which the article defines. The article ends with whatever consonant the following word commences (its final consonant "assimilates" to the following consonant). Thus it has the forms *hak, ham, han*, &c. The article is never written separately from the word which it defines. Thus the final consonant of the article and the initial consonant of the following word are represented by one letter with *daghesh forte* inserted. "The king" is הַמֶּלֶךְ = *hammelekh*.

Gutturals (א, ע, ה, ח), ר and יְ are seldom doubled in Hebrew, and, accordingly, before words commencing with one of these six sounds the article loses its final consonant. In some cases the vowel of the article lengthens in compensation.

Before ה, ח, יְ the form of the article is הַ.

Before א, ע, ר „ „ „ „ הָ.

NOTE.—Another form of the article is הֶ. It is used (1) before words commencing with the syllable חָ (or חֳ); (2) before words commencing with unaccented הָ or עָ (*e.g.* הֶהָמוֹן, הֶהָרִים). No words before which הֶ is required are given until § 13.

The only common exceptions to the rules given in this paragraph are הָהָר, הָהֵם (in all its forms) and הָעִיר. It is usually said that before accented הָ or עָ the form of the article is הָ; but הָהָר is the only case of the occurrence of the article before accented הָ.

Verbs.—The name-form of the verb, *i.e.* the form used in naming it, by which it is referred to, is the 3rd sing. masc. perfect. This part has no termination. It may generally be translated by an English past or perfect (see § 27). The pronominal subject of a verb need not be separately expressed.

The termination of the 1st person sing. perf. is ־תִי. כָּתַבְתִּי is the 1st person sing. of כָּתַב. נוּ is the termination of the 1st person plural. The subject generally follows the verb. When there is an object it comes third. If the accusative is definite, and governed by a transitive verb, it may be preceded by the particle אֶת־.* (See § 24.)

Translation Exercise.

The watchman heard the lion. The lion killed the ass. We wrote a letter. The man sent the book. I heard the ass. He sent the horse. We killed the lion. The king heard the watchman. He stood beside the king.

---

§ 3. THE ARTICLE (*continued*).

After the prepositions בְּ, כְּ, and לְ, the initial ה of the article is elided. These prepositions then lose their own slight vowel (*sh'wa*) and coalesce with the article. בְּהַסּוּס thus becomes בַּסּוּס. Whether before the article or not, these prepositions are not written as separate words, but are joined to the words they precede. In comparisons after כְּ, "like," the Hebrew article is used before a noun which has no attribute attached. As there is no dative in Hebrew, לְ must be used to express an English dative.

Certain words, such as עַם, פַּר, הַר, אֶרֶץ, change their form when combined with the definite article. הָאָרֶץ, הָהָר, הַפָּר, הָעָם are the forms used.

Translation Exercise.

In the well. To the man. Like a king. I did not send the book to the watchman. We wrote in the book. The man heard the lion. He did not slay the ass. The people stood upon the hill. He sent the man an ox.

---

* The stroke following את is the Hebrew hyphen, *makkêph*.

§ 4. ADJECTIVES.

The principal rules of syntax regarding the adjective are:

(1) As an attribute its position is after the noun it qualifies, *e.g.* אִישׁ טוֹב. (2) If the noun has a qualifying article, it must be repeated before the attributive adjective: הָאִישׁ הַטּוֹב. (3) As a predicate the adjective generally follows the subject, but without an article. When the subject is a single noun, and the predicate a single adjective, the predicate often stands first: טוֹב הָאִישׁ or הָאִישׁ טוֹב. (4) The adjective, whether attribute or predicate, agrees with the noun in gender, number (and case).

NOTE.—The second rule is only a particular case of a more general rule, to the effect that a qualifying adjective takes the definite article when the noun it qualifies is definite. Nouns are definite (*a*) if proper names, (*b*) when qualified by the definite article, (*c*) when qualified by a possessive adjective, (*d*) when followed by a genitive which is definite in one of the ways already defined.

The English copulas "is," "are," &c. are generally not expressed by any word in Hebrew; טוֹב הָאִישׁ = "the man is good."

Pathaḥ furtive.—When a word ends in a guttural preceded by a long vowel, not *ḳameṣ*, a *pathaḥ* slips in between the guttural and the preceding vowel to ease the pronunciation. It is written *under* the guttural before which it is pronounced, and is called *pathaḥ furtive*, *e.g.* רוּחַ, גָּבֹהַּ.

TRANSLATION EXERCISE.

A good man. A bad king. The good king. The beautiful daughter. In the good book. To the great king. The watchman is little. The well is large. The small ass is worthless. A good son is a good father. The mountain is high. The country is beautiful.

---

§ 5. THE CONSTRUCT.

A noun which governs another in the genitive is called a construct, or is said to be in the construct state.

NOTE.—Case-*endings* have been almost entirely lost in Hebrew. Generally the case of a noun can only be determined by its function in the sentence. The genitive stands immediately *after* the noun which governs it, *e.g.* רֹאשׁ אִישׁ = "a man's head" (cf. Welsh *pen bachgen*).

The principal rules of syntax regarding the construct* are as follows:

(1) The construct never has an article qualifying it; "the head of the man" is רֹאשׁ הָאִישׁ. (2) Nothing should intervene between a construct and its genitive. Hence an adjective qualifying a construct is placed after the genitive; "the beautiful daughter of the king" is בַּת הַמֶּלֶךְ הַטּוֹבָה. (3) When the construct is definite, the adjective takes the article although the construct does not; rule 1 does not apply to the adjective qualifying a construct. (4) Possession is expressed by a circumlocution (*e.g.* by means of the preposition לְ), and not by a construct and its genitive, when one of the related nouns is definite and the other indefinite. A construct cannot be used with a genitive unless both are definite or both indefinite. Hence the following rule for translating Hebrew into English: if the genitive is definite, the construct must be translated into English with the article; סוּס הַמֶּלֶךְ is "the horse of the king." It is to be observed, however, that the English definite article is often employed before an indefinite genitive, where Hebrew would employ an indefinite noun in both cases. "The daughter of a king" means simply "a king's daughter," and should be so rendered in Hebrew, as it is also in Welsh.

---

* It should be particularly noted, by Welsh students, that rules 1 and 4 are already familiar to them from Welsh idiom. Examples: *mab y brenin, mab brenin, mab i'r brenin.*

Many words in the construct change their form, being hurriedly pronounced. But of the nouns in Vocabularies 1—11 only בֵּן and אָב have special construct forms, בֶּן־ and אֲבִי.

Note.—The construct and the genitive are so closely joined that it is rare to find two constructs before one genitive. The genitive is repeated with each construct, or a pronoun is used in the second case. It is uncommon even to combine several genitives with one construct.

Translation Exercise.

(*a*) A king's head. The voice of the king. The man's son. The watchman's daughter. I heard the voice of the man's son. He wrote in the book of the watchman's father. He did not kill the man's ox. He sent the man's head to the king. The king's good book. The price of the ox. A strong wind.

(*b*) We wrote in the man's book. The beautiful head of the horse. The loud voice of the lion. The roar of the great lion. The king of the country is a very great man. He sent the book to the king's daughter. The hill is very high. The king's beautiful city. The price of an ox. An evil spirit.

---

§ 6. PERSONAL PRONOUNS.

	Nominatives. *Sing.*	Nominatives. *Plur.*	Accusatives. *Sing.*	Accusatives. *Plur.*
1st pers.	אֲנִי or אָנֹכִי	אֲנַחְנוּ, נַחְנוּ (6)	אֹתִי	אֹתָנוּ
2nd pers.	אַתָּה *m.*	אַתֶּם	אֹתְךָ	אֶתְכֶם
,, ,,	אַתְּ *f.*	אַתֵּן (1) or אַתֵּנָה (4)	אֹתָךְ	אֶתְכֶן
3rd pers.	הוּא *m.*	הֵמָּה, הֵם	אֹתוֹ	אֹתָם
,, ,,	הִיא *f.*	הֵנָּה, הֵן	אֹתָהּ	אֹתָן

The pronoun of the 3rd person may be used to express an English copula when the subject is slightly emphatic. English "it" is הוּא or הִיא according to the gender of the Hebrew noun. The figures in brackets give the number of occurrences in the O.T.

The conjunction "and" has various forms in Hebrew. וְ is most usual; וּ is used before בּ, ו, מ and פּ, and before any consonant followed by vocal *sh'wa* simple; preceding a consonant followed by a *ḥateph* the short vowel corresponding to the *ḥateph* is the vowel of the conjunction, hence the forms וַ, וֶ, וָ; *e.g.* סוּס וַאֲרִי. וָ = *wā* is employed before the accent, especially between pairs of closely connected words, *e.g.* חֲמוֹר וָסוּס.

Translation Exercise.

(*a*) I am good. He is the great king. He heard me. We heard them. I sent him. She is little and he is tall. He sent them to the well. You are tall. We are small. The lion killed the ox on the hill. He is king of a great people. They are tall. It is a great price.

(*b*) You and I are little. We and they are good. I heard a lion and an ass. He is good and great. He sent you and me to the man's daughter. We did not hear the sound. We stood beside the well in the beautiful city.

---

§ 7. PERSONAL PRONOUNS (*continued*).

The genitives of the personal pronouns, which are expressed in English by the possessive adjectives "my," "thy," &c., are expressed in Hebrew by suffixes.

my horse	סוּסִי	our horse	סוּסֵנוּ	to me	לִי	to us	נוּ
thy (*m.*) "	סוּסְךָ	your (*m.*) "	סוּסְכֶם	to thee (*m.*)	לְךָ	to you (*m.*)	כֶם
thy (*f.*) "	סוּסֵךְ	your (*f.*) "	סוּסְכֶן	to thee (*f.*)	לָךְ	to you (*f.*)	כֶן
his "	סוּסוֹ	their (*m.*) "	סוּסָם	to him	לוֹ	to them (*m.*)	הֶם
her "	סוּסָהּ	their (*f.*) "	סוּסָן	to her	לָהּ	to them (*f.*)	הֶן

All prepositions in Hebrew govern the genitive case. Hence pronominal suffixes are always employed with prepositions to express a pronominal object; "to him" is לוֹ.

The combinations לִי, לְךָ &c. are used to express the possessive pronouns "mine," "thine," &c. But such a sentence as "Your horse is like mine," where the pronoun is itself governed by a preposition, must be translated סוּסְךָ כְּסוּסִי.

There is no verb "to have" in Hebrew. "I have" is rendered by לִי, "thou hast" by לְךָ, &c.

NOTE.—*Sh'wa,* in the suffixes ־ְךָ, ־ְכֶם, ־ְכֶן, will be ־ֲ when the final consonant of the noun is a guttural. After gutturals *sh'wa* vocal always becomes *ḥateph,* and generally *ḥateph pathaḥ.* ־ָם and ־ָן come from older forms ־הֶם and ־הֶן, still sometimes used (*e.g.* with certain prepositions). The nouns to which suffixes are attached frequently change their form in consequence. But until § 18 only unchangeable nouns are given in the Exercises. When ־ְךָ is in pause, *i.e.* at the end of a sentence or elsewhere when the voice makes a considerable stop, it is written and pronounced ־ֶךָ.

TRANSLATION EXERCISE.

(*a*) His voice is loud. Her husband is in the city. He sent her to the well. He wrote a letter to her. He sent it to me. The watchman heard me. The land is yours. Our horse is a good one. Their ass is worthless.

(*b*) The country belongs to us. I have the ox. We have the horse's head. The man's daughter has the book. The ox is hers. Your husband is like mine. His horse and her ass. He sent an evil spirit amongst them.

---

§ 8. DEMONSTRATIVE PRONOUNS.

This	זֶה (*m.*)	That	הוּא (*m.*)	Those	הֵמָּה, הֵם
,,	זֹאת (*f.*)	,,	הִיא (*f.*)	,,	הֵנָּה, הֵן
These	אֵלֶּה				

זֶה is not inflected for case. הוּא is inflected exactly like the personal pronoun הוּא.

When "this" has a neuter sense, denoting an event or mode of conduct, it is translated by זֹאת; but neuter "that" is translated הוּא.

These pronouns are also used as demonstative adjectives, and are then treated like adjectives, standing after the noun they qualify and taking the article. The noun they qualify also takes the definite article, unless, of course, it is a construct or has a pronominal suffix attached to it. Ex.: הַסּוּס הַטּוֹב הַזֶּה. The form of the article before הֵם and the other words for "those" is הָ (§ 2, Note).

NOTE.—When a noun has a pronominal suffix attached, and is also qualified by a demonstrative, the demonstrative need not have the article prefixed.

TRANSLATION EXERCISE.

This is large. That is very small. These are good. Those are very bad. This well. That city. That hill is high. This ox is mine. That country belongs to the king. My father gave me that book. He wrote this in the man's book. I am the king of this country. I know that. He placed it upon his head. We heard her voice. This beautiful land is his.

---

§ 9. RELATIVE PRONOUN.

The relative אֲשֶׁר does not vary its form for gender, number, or case. As a pure relative, however, it is never employed in the genitive case. It cannot therefore be placed under the government of a preposition. "The man to whom he gave the book" is הָאִישׁ אֲשֶׁר נָתַן הַסֵּפֶר לוֹ (cf. Welsh, *y ty y ganwyd ef ynddo*). A "resumptive" pronoun is often used even when the relative is an accusative. "The man whom he killed" may be הָאִישׁ אֲשֶׁר הָרַג אֹתוֹ.

In combination with שָׁם, שָׁמָּה, and מִשָּׁם, אֲשֶׁר expresses the relative adverbs "where," "whither," "whence." הָהָר אֲשֶׁר

שָׁם שָׁמַע אֶת־הַקּוֹל "the hill where he heard the voice." Combined with prepositions it forms conjunctions; עַד־אֲשֶׁר is the conjunction "until."

NOTE.—אֲשֶׁר is also employed to express "he who," "they who," "that which," &c. When so used it is found in the genitive case; לַאֲשֶׁר "to him who," בַּאֲשֶׁר "by that which," &c. (For לַ and בַּ, see § 11.)

TRANSLATION EXERCISE.

The man to whom I gave this horse. The watchman whom I sent to you. The country to which he went. That is what he gave me. I have kept the book in which I wrote. The country whence he went out. He stood beside the well until the morning. I watched the ox until my father sent me there.

---

§ 10. INTERROGATIVE PRONOUNS.

Of persons מִי is employed as nominative and genitive, אֶת־מִי as the accusative. In order to have the sense of "whose?" מִי must occupy the genitive position after a noun; *e.g.* בֶּן־מִי הוּא "whose son is he." When there is no governing word, לְמִי is used for "whose?"; לְמִי הַפָּר "whose is the ox?" Whether nominative or accusative the interrogative stands first in a sentence.

Of things מָה, מֶה or מַה־ is employed, without distinction of case. (1) מָה is used standing independently, also before the article, before הֵם, &c., and before all words commencing with א or ר. (2) מֶה before words commencing with חָ, עָ or הָ (exclusive of the article). (3) מַה־ before הוּא and הִיא, and before words which do not commence with a guttural or ר. The close union between מַה־ and non-gutturals is marked by the insertion of (conjunctive) *daghesh*; hence מַה־זֹּאת.

NOTE.—מִי and מָה sometimes correspond to the English indefinite relatives "whoever," "whatever." "Which?" happens to occur only rarely in the Old Testament; it is expressed by אֵי זֶה (literally "where?").—מה before ח, ע and ה rarely occurs except as provided for in the above rules; before ע and ה the forms מֶה and מָה are then used; before ח, מֶה and also מַה־. מֶה sometimes occurs before non-gutturals (*e.g.* before קוֹל). After prepositions either מֶה or מָה is used (hence עַל־מָה and עַל־מֶה; בַּמָּה occurs independently and before א or ה, בַּמֶּה in other connections). מֶה־ and מָה־ are less usual than מֶה and מָה.

Translation Exercise.

What is this? What is that? What is that man? What are these? I do not know who they are. Whom did he send? To whom did he give that book? Whose daughter is she? Whose is this? Who killed this ox? Who went to them? What did he give us? What is that sound? What are those?

---

§ 11. PREPOSITIONS WITH VARIABLE FORMS.

בְּ, כְּ and לְ, usually pronounced with hurried vowels, retain in some cases (the older) more distinct vowels.

(1) Before consonants followed by simple *sh'wa* vocal, they have the forms בִּ, כִּ, לִ.

(2) Before consonants followed by a *ḥaṭeph*, they have a short vowel corresponding to the *ḥaṭeph* (hence in לַאֲשֶׁר the form is לַ, and the forms לֶ and לָ also occur).

Note.—In certain cases the vowel of these prepositions is *ḳameṣ*; לָ is used before monosyllabic and segholate infinitives, and in the compound לָמָּה "why?" (לָמָה before א, ה, and ע).

Regarding מִן־ the following rules must be observed: (1) The primary form is employed only before the article, and then not always. (2) In general the final *n* assimilates to the initial consonant of the word following, *i.e.* the preposition becomes *mis-*, *mit-*, &c. according to the consonant it precedes. (3) Before gutturals and ר the form מֵ is used (or sometimes מִ). Exx. מֵרֹאשׁ, מִסֵּפֶר.

Translation Exercise.

(*a*) In a book. In the book. To a man. To the man. From there. From a high hill. Like a horse. Why did he send her to the city? He went out from the city in the morning. Your ass is like mine. He gave it to the king's daughter. He sent her husband a horse and an ass. He is like the king of the country. This well is ours. To whom did he write that letter?

(*b*) He went there every day. He came out of the well in the morning. We stood there all the day. The people did not know. I sent her the watchman. He bought it at a great price. Why did he kill their horse? To-day is a great day in the city. This is our ass. It is my well. What is it?

---

§ 12. GENDER AND CASE

(of nouns and adjectives).

There are two genders, masculine and feminine. Things that are lifeless are grammatically either masculine or feminine. Some nouns are of common gender.

Parts of the body and instruments are generally feminine. But רֹאשׁ, אַף, פֶּה, לֵב are masculine (see vocabulary 12).

Special feminine terminations are ־ָה, and ת preceded by a variety of vowels (as in מַקֶּבֶת "hammer"). ־ָה represents an original ־ָת or ־ַת, and this is retained (1) in the construct (־ַת), (2) with pronominal suffixes (־ָת or ־ַת), (3) with the dual termination (־ָת).

Hebrew nouns should be parsed as nominative, genitive or accusative according to their function in the sentence; but the old case-endings have been practically lost, and the forms of nouns therefore do not vary in accordance with their case. The old accusative ending ־ָה survives more often than the nominative and genitive endings (ו or ו and ־ִי). It is frequently attached to accusatives that express motion towards (cf. שָׁמָּה from שָׁם). Unlike the feminine ־ָה it is unaccented. (See § 22, Note *d.*)

Translation Exercise.

My teaching. His teaching. Thy teaching. His wisdom. This great possession. This is my commandment. The wall of that city. He obeyed my commandment. The wisdom of the king is very great. This land is the property of that people. Whose wisdom is like his? He went from there towards the hill.

---

§ 13. FIRST DECLENSION.

Nouns and adjectives may be divided into "declensions" according to the changes which the stem-syllables undergo when terminations are attached. When a termination adds to the number of syllables in a word and receives the accent, as it generally does, the vowels at the beginning of the word are necessarily hurried over somewhat. This is specially the case with penultimate *ḳameṣ* and *ṣere,* and their hurried pronunciation is represented in writing by *sh'wa.* Words in which penultimate *ḳameṣ* or *ṣere* becomes vocal *sh'wa,* when an accented termination is attached, may be called first declension nouns. (If the *sh'wa* follow a guttural it must be a *ḥaṭeph,* and is generally ־ֲ).

The feminine singular of adjectives is generally formed by the addition of ־ָה to the masculine singular. Penultimate *ḳameṣ* or *ṣere* in general then becomes vocal *sh'wa* (see vocab. 4).

Regarding the form of the article before הָ see § 2, Note.

Translation Exercise.

A mighty wind. That strong man. This wise king. That new wall. This wall is very high. The commandment of the king is good. She is good and great. His head is small. The wall of the city is high. We gave her a horse and an ass. A new commandment I have given to you. He gave them a spirit of wisdom.

---

§ 14. NUMBER.

There are three numbers, singular, plural, and dual. The dual is hardly used except to express the English plural of nouns which naturally occur in pairs, as hands, feet, &c. An adjective agreeing with a dual is put in the plural. The terminations are :—

Masc. plur.	Fem. plur.	Dual.
ִים (constr. ֵי)	וֹת	ַיִם (constr. ֵי)

Rules for Inflection.—Singulars which end in ָה or ֶה drop these terminations when a plural ending is attached. No further change then takes place; תּוֹרָה, plural תּוֹרוֹת.

In the case of other words, where the addition of the termination increases the number of the syllables, first declension nouns inflect as already described (§ 13). Hence דָּבָר, plural דְּבָרִים. The same change also occurs in the dual of feminines in ָה, where the final syllable is preserved in the form ָת. The dual of שָׂפָה (=שָׂפָת) is שְׂפָתַיִם.

Note.—Masculine nouns sometimes have plurals in וֹת (*e.g.* שָׂדֶה, קוֹל, לֵב, אָב, שֵׁם, מִזְבֵּחַ), and feminine nouns plurals in ִים (*e.g.* שָׁנָה).

Translation Exercise.

I did not know these things. Those holy prophets. They are righteous. You are good and great. The shepherd watched the sheep in the fields. Small hands. The beautiful hands. These asses are small. Those are the shepherds. The old prophets. The commandments of the righteous king. The horses of my father. The shepherds of this country. The asses of the shepherd's son. What is the price of the field?

---

§ 15. COMPARISON OF ADJECTIVES.

There are no terminations to express the degree of an adjective. The simple form is used also for the comparative and superlative. When comparative in sense it is followed by מִן־ ("away from") = "than." When superlative the article is often prefixed.

In comparative sentences "older," "oldest," "younger" "youngest," are expressed by גָּדוֹל and קָטוֹן.

Some nouns are used in the plural only, particularly abstract nouns (see vocabulary 15). אֱלֹהִים is a plural, but construed as a singular. מַיִם and שָׁמַיִם are plurals although dual in form. Instead of לֶאֱלֹהִים the contracted form לֵאלֹהִים is always used, and similar contraction takes place after בְּ, כְּ, and וְ (see also § 20).

Translation Exercise.*

He is taller than the king. This well is larger than ours. He obeyed the commandment of the prophet. This wall is the highest. The man's youngest son is in the field. This is the eldest. She is the eldest daughter. He is older than I. He is the worst. All these horses are from us. The wisdom of God is greater than the wisdom of man. Youth and old age. Heaven and earth belong to God. The life of the righteous is in his hand.

---

§ 16. SPECIAL CONSTRUCT FORMS.

Words in the construct frequently take special forms. A construct is always combined closely in pronunciation with the

* See table for מִן with pronominal suffixes.

following genitive. As a consequence, on the one hand it is pronounced more hurriedly than when independent (*in statu absoluto*), and on the other hand it is less exposed to phonetic change. Hence the special construct forms are somewhat archaic as well as hurriedly pronounced.

Variations of the Construct in Final Syllables.—The principal cases are these: the endings ־ִים and ־ַיִם become ־ֵי in the construct (§ 14); for ־ָה the older ־ַת is employed (§ 12); ־ֶה is replaced by ־ֵה; and every *ḳameṣ* in a final syllable reverts to (an older) *pathaḥ* (unless the word ends in ־ָא).

Translation Exercise.

The righteous of the earth are God's possession. God's holy prophets are the shepherds of the people. I do not know the captain of the army. The commandment of God is holy. He stood before the king. The shepherd went before his sheep. The king's shepherd has a son and a daughter. All the people pursued the army on that day. They are in the hand of God.

---

§ 17. CONSTRUCT FORMS (*continued*).

Variations of Penultimate Syllables.—If the vowel of the penultimate be unaccented *ḳameṣ* or *ṣere* it becomes a vocal *sh'wa* in the construct; *e.g.* קָדוֹשׁ becomes קְדוֹשׁ, חָצִיר becomes חֲצִיר.

When a vocal *sh'wa* precedes this penultimate syllable there is another change also: Not only does *ḳameṣ* or *ṣere* become vocal *sh'wa*, the preceding *sh'wa* simple is replaced by *ḥireḳ* (see below).

Many words, naturally, are subject to change both in the final syllable (§ 16), and in the penultimate. So, for example, dissyllabic words with *ḳameṣ* in both syllables; the construct of דָּבָר is דְּבַר, that of שָׂפָה is שְׂפַת. Very many plurals also necessarily change in both syllables; the construct of פָּנִים is פְּנֵי, that of שָׁמַיִם is שְׁמֵי. Illustrations of the three possible changes are given by plurals and feminines like דְּבָרִים and נְקָמָה, of which the constructs are דִּבְרֵי and נִקְמַת.

Translation Exercise.

The word of the man of God. All flesh is like the grass of the field. The vengeance of the shepherd's son. The blood of the righteous is upon the face of the earth. The judgments of God are good. He sent the elders of the city to the prophet. The holy words of God's revelation. He pursued after the king's army. The words of the holy prophet are upon the king's lips every day.

---

§ 18. PRONOMINAL SUFFIXES

(INFLECTION OF SINGULAR NOUNS).

The forms of the suffixes have been given in § 7. For the purpose of the following rules they are divided into light and heavy. Heavy suffixes are those containing two consonants.

Rules of Inflection.—(1) When the suffix is light penultimate *ḳameṣ* or *ṣere* (unaccented) becomes vocal *sh'wa*; *e.g.* דְּבָרִי "my word" from דָּבָר.

(2) When the suffix is heavy the noun takes a construct form (*i.e.* change takes place both in the penultimate and in the final syllable according to the rules of § 17); *e.g.* דִּבְרְכֶם "your word."

In either case vocal *sh'wa* simple preceding the penultimate syllable becomes *ḥireḳ* according to § 17.

These rules apply to feminines in ־ָה, with the proviso that the original ending in ־ַת is restored; נִקְמָתִי "my vengeance."

Note.—Nouns ending in ־ֶה lose their termination when suffixes are attached, and so when the suffixes are light do not change the other stem-vowels, *e.g.* שָׂדֵנוּ "our field." The uncontracted suffixes ־ֵהוּ and ־ָהּ are generally used with these nouns for "his" and "her."

Translation Exercise.

My flesh. His lip. Our word. Their judgment. Her blood. Your (*f.*) judgment. His shepherd. Your (*m.*) flesh. Thy prophet. My field. Thy commandment. Your (*m.*) commandment. His wisdom. Their great possession. Her good shepherd. My holy prophet. This is my ass. It is his voice. This good land is the king's. He put his hand upon her head. His day of vengeance.

---

§ 19. PRONOMINAL SUFFIXES

(WITH PLURALS AND DUALS).

		Plural in ־ִים.		*Plural in* וֹת.	
1st pers.	(*c.*)	סוּסַי	סוּסֵינוּ	מִצְוֹתַי	מִצְוֹתֵינוּ
2nd ,,	(*m.*)	סוּסֶיךָ	סוּסֵיכֶם	מִצְוֹתֶיךָ	מִצְוֹתֵיכֶם
,, ,,	(*f.*)	סוּסַיִךְ	סוּסֵיכֶן	מִצְוֹתַיִךְ	מִצְוֹתֵיכֶן
3rd ,,	(*m.*)	סוּסָיו	סוּסֵיהֶם	מִצְוֹתָיו	מִצְוֹתֵיהֶם
,, ,,	(*f.*)	סוּסֶיהָ	סוּסֵיהֶן	מִצְוֹתֶיהָ	מִצְוֹתֵיהֶן

The accent in these forms is on the connective vowels (see below), except in heavy suffixes. In ־ָיו *yodh* is silent.

(*a*) **Rules for the Inflection of Plurals in ־ִים and Duals.**

(1) Light suffixes are united to the independent form of the plural and of the dual, being substituted for the terminations ־ִים and ־ַיִם; *e.g.* דְּבָרַי "my words," from דְּבָרִים.

(2) Heavy suffixes are united to the construct form, being substituted for the termination ־ֵי; *e.g.* דִּבְרֵיכֶם from דִּבְרֵי (construct of דְּבָרִים).

NOTE.—In the suffixes ־ֶיךָ, ־ֵינוּ, &c., the vowels ־ֶי, ־ֵי, &c. are termed connective vowels. They are really the plural termination of the noun itself, and the pronominal suffix is only ךָ, נוּ, &c., exactly as in the singular. It is simpler, however, for the beginner to assume that the vowels are part of the pronominal suffix, and the Hebrews themselves treated them as such by joining them to words which already had a plural ending of their own in וֹת, *e.g.* מִצְוֹתֵינוּ.

(*b*) **Inflections of Plurals in** וֹת. The termination וֹת is retained, and the suffixes light and heavy produce (necessarily) the same effect: penultimate *ḳames* or *ṣere* becomes vocal *sh'wa.* If there be a *sh'wa* preceding this penultimate syllable, it then becomes *ḥireḳ*; hence נִקְמוֹתָיו. Instead of the suffixes ־ֵיהֶם and ־ֵיהֶן, older forms without the intrusive masculine plural ending are also found; *e.g.* מִצְוֹתָם.

Translation Exercise.

Her words. My face. Our God. Thine instructions. Our hands. Thy fields. His lips. Their shepherds. Their face. His great ones. My little ones. God is good to his saints. He set it before all the people. He observed God's commands from his youth to his old age. What is this new teaching? The day of vengeance of our God.

---

§ 20. PREPOSITIONS WITH PLURAL SUFFIXES.

Hebrew prepositions seem for the most part to have been originally nouns. Some are plainly plurals in origin, *e.g.* לִפְנֵי from פָּנִים; others are treated according to the analogy of plurals. Of prepositions which require plural suffixes, אֶל־ and עַל־ are the most common. With suffixes they use as their basal forms אֵל and עָל (see table). Suffixes are attached to לִפְנֵי according to the rules that would apply to פָּנִים. Hence לְפָנַי "before me," from פָּנַי "my face."

For "the Lord," as applied to God, Hebrew uses אֲדֹנָי "my Lord" (see vocabulary 20). לַאֲדֹנָי contracts to לַאדֹנָי (comp. § 15). Similar contraction always takes place after וְ, כְּ, בְּ, and מְ, when a word commences with יְ; לְיְהוּדָה becomes לִיהוּדָה.

Translation Exercise.

Before us. Before you. Upon it. Upon them. After thee. He stood beside me. He went before him all that day. He did not hearken unto the words of the prophet. I do not know the man to whom he has gone. He pursued after him until he stood beside the well. Our life is in his hand. His master sent him to the city. My Lord and my God. The Lord is king over all the earth.

---

§ 21. SECOND DECLENSION.

(~~See~~ Segholate Nouns).

These nouns are dissyllables with the accent on the first syllable, *e.g.* סֵפֶר, אֶרֶץ. Originally they were monosyllables ending in two consonants; but a helping vowel has slipped in between the final consonants to ease pronunciation (cf. Welsh *pobol* from *pobl*). The helping vowel is generally *s·ghol*, hence the name Segholates.

Classification.—The Segholates may be classified according to the vowel of the original monosyllable into an *ă* class, an *ĭ* class, and an *ŏ* class. In each case the original vowel is usually affected by the insertion of the helping vowel, so that the dissyllabic forms of the three classes are exemplified by מֶלֶךְ, סֵפֶר, בֹּקֶר (from מַלְכּ, סִפְר, and בָּקְר respectively).

Rule for Inflection.—Singulars and duals when inflected take their original monosyllabic form. Plurals are treated according to the analogy of דָבָר, except that in each class the *sh·wa* preceding the antepenultimate syllable, before another *sh·wa* simple, is replaced by the short vowel of the class (*a*, *i*, or *o*), and not by *ḥireḳ* (*i*) alone.

Note.—Feminines in ־ָה like מַלְכָּה, שִׁפְחָה, נַעֲרָה, also form their plurals according to the analogy of דָבָר (מְלָכוֹת, &c.), and not according to the rule of § 14. They may be regarded as derived from monosyllabic stems.

Construct.—In the singular, the independent and the construct forms of Segholates are generally alike.

TRANSLATION EXERCISE.

His country. Our king. Her kindness. My foot. Our kings. My ear. Our ears. Their bread. His kindnesses. Your feet. His sanctuary. Our queen. Their queens. His kindness is new every morning. My king and my God. He stood in the sanctuary from morning until evening. The heaven of heavens is the Lord's, and the earth he has given to us. Their ways are very evil. My ways are not your ways.

---

§ 22. SEGHOLATES (*continued*).

Some nouns which resemble מֶלֶךְ in their dissyllabic forms have *ḥireḳ* as the vowel of their monosyllabic form. Exx. צֶדֶק, בֶּרֶךְ, פֶּתַח, זֶבַח.

Besides מֶלֶךְ there are three other types belonging to the ă class, with certain peculiarities of inflection. (Exx. נַעַר, זַיִת, מָוֶת.) (*a*) When the medial consonant is a guttural, the stem to which the suffix is attached is not always strictly monosyllabic; *ḥaṭeph pathaḥ* frequently slips in after the guttural (particularly ע). Hence נַעֲרוֹ, but לַחְמוֹ. (*b*) When the medial consonant is י or ו, the monosyllabic stem is usually employed in plurals, as well as in singulars and duals, and this stem is used in the construct also. זֵית and מוֹת are the monosyllabic types of these classes (from זַיְת and מַוְת).

Many trisyllabic nouns have a segholate ending, which is inflected as if it were a segholate noun. Hence מַקַּבְתִּי, from מַקֶּבֶת. Feminine trisyllables like מַמְלָכָה have a segholate form in the construct and with suffixes; מַמְלֶכֶת עוֹלָם "kingdom of eternity" = everlasting kingdom.

NOTES.—(*a*) Some nouns of the third class in the plural, after initial guttural or ק, have ֳ as their hurried vowel. Exx. קֳדָשִׁים, הָאֳהָלִים.

(*b*) Others retain *ó* as the initial vowel; אֳהָלִים is used without prefixes, and light pronominal suffixes are joined to this form.

(*c*) Nouns like גְּדִי are treated like Segholates; hence גְּדְיוֹ "his kid," גְּדָיִים "kids." In the construct plural of this type the *ḳameṣ* is unalterable; גְּדָיֵי.

(*d*) The accusative ending ־ָה, being unaccented, usually exercises no influence on the form of the nouns to which it is attached. In the case of Segholates, however, when the accusative ending is added, the helping vowel is hurriedly pronounced and written vocal *sh'wa*. In the case of אַרְצָה and חַדְרָה (from חֶדֶר "a chamber"), the original stem-vowel is retained. The accusative form לַיְלָה, from לַיִל "night," has supplanted the nominative and genitive in ordinary use (construct, לֵיל; plural, לֵילוֹת).

Translation Exercise.

My righteousness. His knee. Their knees. Her death. Your olive tree. Thy sacrifices. The gate of the city. The king's house. The sacrifices of God. The death of the righteous. The house of God is holy. He went to his house. The gates of the city. Life and death are in the hand of God. His kingdom is an everlasting kingdom. He was a man of war from his youth. He went out to battle against the people. He is righteous in God's sight. The eyes of the Lord are upon the evil and the good.

---

§ 23. THIRD DECLENSION.

Third declension nouns are nouns of two or more syllables, in which the vowel of the final syllable is *ṣere* and the penultimate vowel is not *ḳameṣ*. (Such nouns as בְּאֵר are not included by the definition; see page 6.)

Rule for Inflection.—*Ṣere* becomes vocal *sh'wa*, except where the suffix following has *sh'wa* as its connective vowel; before such suffixes *ṣere* is replaced (usually) by a short vowel, generally *s'ghol*, *ḥireḳ* under the influence of י, *pathaḥ* under the influence of a guttural. Exx. שֹׁפְטִים, שֹׁפֶטְךָ, אֹיִבְךָ, מִזְבַּחֲךָ (see vocabulary).

The Construct in the singular is generally the same as the independent form, but in some cases *ṣere* is replaced by *pathaḥ*. The change is confined to such nouns as have a preformative מ (denoting place, instrument, &c.).

Two monosyllables (בֵּן "son," and שֵׁם "a name") in the singular belong to this declension. Their *ṣere* becomes *sh'wa* or *ḥireḳ* according to the suffix attached; *e.g.* בְּנִי, בִּנְךָ. Their constructs are בֶּן־ and שֵׁם; their plurals, בָּנִים and שֵׁמוֹת.

NOTE.—Certain nouns whose final vowel is *ḥolem* or *ḳameṣ* (such as participles Niph'al) are inflected in the plural according to this declension; *e.g.* אַרְמְנוֹת and צִפֳּרִים, from אַרְמוֹן ("tower") and צִפּוֹר ("bird"). So also the plurals of some nouns with a segholate ending of the ŏ class; *e.g.* גֻּלְגֹּלֶת "skull," plural גֻּלְגְּלוֹת.

TRANSLATION EXERCISE.

(*a*) My enemy. My priests. His enemies. His priests. Their judges. Your priests. Her mourning. My altar. Thine altar. Your (f.) judge. His name. Our enemies. This righteous judge. This judge is righteous. The judge of my righteousness. The righteousness of those judges.

(*b*) The mourning of the people was very great. The judge of all the earth is righteous. The names of the righteous are written in the book of life. The prophet sent them to the priest. His name is great in all the earth. He stood beside the altar of God. The enemies of our country. He sacrificed sacrifices upon the altars. His son did not hear his voice nor keep his commandments. His anger is more bitter than death.

§ 24. FOURTH DECLENSION.

The nouns of this declension are not easily defined. They are predominantly monosyllabic, and include all whose vowel is *pathaḥ*, many whose vowel is *ṣere*, and one class of monosyllables in *ḥolem* (spelled like חֹק not like קוֹל).

Rule for Inflection.—The final radical is doubled when a termination is attached; in the second class, *ṣere* shortens to *ḥireḳ*; and in the third, *ḥolem* shortens to ֻ. Exx. עַמִּים, חִצִּים, חֻקִּים, from עַם, חֵץ, חֹק.

If the final consonant be a guttural, or ר, doubling cannot take place. In such cases *pathaḥ* is frequently lengthened to *ḳameṣ* in compensation; *e.g.* הַר, plural הָרִים. Compensation *ḳameṣ* never becomes vocal *sh'wa*; hence הָרֵי is the construct of הָרִים.

Construct.—In the construct singular of the third class the vowel *ḥolem* shortens to ָ, and the word is joined to the following by *maḳḳeph*; *e.g.* חָק־ from חֹק. The other classes generally remain unchanged in the construct singular.

NOTE.—The accusative particle אֵת, and the preposition אֵת "with," usually appear in a construct form אֶת־ (cf. אֶל־, as if from אֵל). עַם with suffixes is treated like a noun of this declension; hence עִמִּי "with me," &c. There are also first declension nouns whose final syllable is treated as if they belonged to this declension; *e.g.* גָּמָל ("camel"), plural גְּמַלִּים; אָדוֹם ("red"), plural אֲדֻמִּים. First declension nouns ending in ִי double the י before an inflectional ending; *e.g.* עָנִי, plural עֲנִיִּים.

TRANSLATION EXERCISE.

His people. Many peoples. His arrows. My decree. Her mother. His voice. Our ox. All of it. All of them. God's decrees are righteous. The hills of the country are very high. The king's arrows are in the heart of his enemies. The people of this land did not obey God's commandments. His ox and his ass and all that he has. These waters are bitter. The sound of many waters is in my ears. The hills of this land and its trees.

---

§ 25. NOUNS WITH VARIABLE STEMS.

A list of the most common of these nouns is given in Vocabulary 25. It is to be observed that the original stem may be found in the plural (רָאשׁ is older than רֹאשׁ). Regarding בָּתִּים, see note page 3. The penultimate *kameṣ* in בָּתִּים, עָרִים and רָאשִׁים is unchangeable; hence construct בָּתֵּי, &c. The construct of אַחִים is אֲחֵי (as if from אָחִים). The plural of פֶּה is rare, and varies in its form. Hebrew often uses the singular of פֶּה where idiomatic English requires a plural.

---

§ 26. NOUNS WITH VARIABLE STEMS (*continued*).

For the forms with pronominal suffixes see Table 14. If the stem ends in a vowel, the suffix no longer requires a connective vowel. אָב, אָח, and פֶּה employ the forms אבי, אחי, and פִּי in the construct and with suffixes. אָבִיו is a contraction for אָבִיהוּ; אָבִי may also be a contraction. אֶחָיו for אַחָיו exemplifies the regular phonetic change of *paṭhaḥ* before ח (compare the article הֶ for הַ, § 2). אִשָּׁה is אֵשֶׁת in the construct and with suffixes. בִּתֵּי &c. for בַּתֵּי &c. again illustrates the tendency of *paṭhaḥ* to change (to ĕ and ĭ). מַיִם with suffixes is treated like זַיִת, *i.e.*, the plural ם is retained; but the construct is generally מֵי.

Translation Exercise.

His father and his mother. Her son and her daughter. My wife and my brothers. My sons and my daughters. The houses of the city. The cities of the land. His brothers. Her husbands. The days of my life. The mouth of his enemy. The hill where I heard the voices (§ 14). What are these cities, my brother?

§ 27. THE VERB.

Every Hebrew verb may have three forms: simple, intensive, and causative. They are known as Ḳal, Pi'êl, and Hiph'îl, respectively. They are all active voices, and may each have a corresponding passive and reflexive. Hence the scheme of the Hebrew verb is:

	Active	*Passive*	*Reflexive*
Simple . .	Ḳal	—	Niph'al
Intensive . .	Pi'êl	Pu'al	Hithpa'êl
Causative . .	Hiph'îl	Hoph'al	—

In this scheme two forms are wanting: the passive Ḳal, and the reflexive Hiph'il. For the former, the Niph'al is employed; for the latter, one of the two existing reflexives.

Each form has five principal parts: perfect, imperfect, imperative (except in passives), infinitives, and participles. The perfect denotes complete action, and the imperfect incomplete action. They are therefore not properly tenses (=verb-forms expressing distinctions of time). Both may be translated by English pasts, presents, or futures; but most actions regarded as complete are past.

קָטַל is the typical form of the 3rd sing. masc. perfect Ḳal. The names of the other forms are so constructed as to give the vowels and preformative syllables of the 3rd sing. masc. perfect of each form. (They are really the actual forms of the verb פָּעַל, *e.g.* נִפְעַל.) The intensives regularly double the middle radical. Hence the perfect Pi'el of קָטַל is קִטֵּל, the perfect Niph'al is נִקְטַל, &c. (see Table).

NOTES.—(*a*) The perfects Ḳal of stative verbs (denoting a state) may have *ē* or *ō* as their second vowel. (*b*) Some of the forms of verbs final guttural require *pathaḥ* furtive; *e.g.* הִשְׁלִיחַ. (*c*) Some Pi'els have *ă* instead of *ē* as their second vowel; *e.g.* לִמַּד, גִּדַּל, קִדַּשׁ, and verbs final guttural. (*d*) Some Pi'els have a causative force; *e.g.* לִמֵּד "teach." (*e*) Regarding the Hithpa'el of verbs initial sibilant, see § 37.

EXERCISE.

Form the seven perfects of the verbs given in Vocabulary 27.

---

§ 28. PERFECTS ḲAL AND NIPH'AL.

For the forms see Table. The vowel terminations ָה and וּ, and the heavy terminations תֶּם and תֶּן, are accented. In stative verbs an English present is translated by the Hebrew perfect. "It is holy," is קָדַשׁ. States are often expressed in English by verbs which are passive in form (see vocabulary).

TRANSLATION EXERCISE.

They are honoured. We grew up. It is bound. You have taught. His name is great upon the earth. He was honoured in the eyes of the people. His hand was heavy against them. He tended his father's sheep. She tied it upon his hand. They wrote God's commandments and ordinances in the book of instruction. The Lord in his anger punished him.

---

§ 29. OTHER PERFECTS.

For the forms see Table. The change of *ē* and *ī* when terminations are attached should be noted (קִטַּלְתָּ from קִטֵּל, הִקְטַלְתָּ from הִקְטִיל), and the retention of the accentuated stem-vowel in הִקְטִילָה and הִקְטִילוּ (cf. קָטְלָה, &c.)

Many verbs are not used in the Ḳal (see vocabulary 29). When the only active is a Hiphil, the passive may be a Niphal. Reciprocal actions are expressed by the Niphal. דִּבֶּר has ֶ in the 3rd sing. masc. perfect only.

TRANSLATION EXERCISE.

She spoke. They divided. We divided. We fought. You destroyed. Thou didst seek. I have consecrated. They sought his life. They fought against him. They divided their property. He honoured his father and his mother. Who destroyed this city? They are destroyed by the wrath of his anger. He was honoured by his people all the days of his life.

---

§ 30. IMPERFECT TENSES.

(3RD SING. MASC.)

The imperfects are formed from the 3rd sing. masc. perfect by prefixing a preformative syllable (see Table). But initial נ of the Niphal is assimilated to the stem, and the initial ה of the Hiphil, Hophal, and Hithpael is elided. The various preformative vowels should be specially noted. Stative verbs and verbs final guttural have *pathaḥ* as the stem-vowel of the imperfect Ḳal (are "imperfects in *pathaḥ*"); *e.g.* יִכְבַּד.

EXERCISE.

Form the imperfects of the various verbs given in vocabularies 27 and 29.

---

§ 31. IMPERFECT TENSES (*continued*).

The masculine forms (as given in Table) are most easily learned separately. The plural termination ו is not required in the 1st person, since the consonant of the preformative syllable (נ) is not the same as in the singular (א). The preformative vowel of the 1st person singular is not always the same as that of the 3rd person; *ḥireḳ* becomes *s·ghol,* and simple vocal *sh·wa* becomes *ḥaṭeph pathaḥ,* both under the influence of initial א (*e.g.* אֶקְטֹל, אֲקַטֵּל). ִ◌י of the imperfect Hiphil is retained before the plural termination וּ, as in the perfect (§ 29).

Translation Exercise.

He writes. They write. You write. I write. I shall teach. You will consecrate. Thou shalt seek. She will speak. I will swear. He will fight. They will fight. They will destroy. It will be destroyed. You will divide.

---

§ 32. JUSSIVES AND COHORTATIVES.

The imperfect frequently expresses commands or exhortations. This is called its jussive or cohortative use. There are no imperative forms for the 1st and 3rd persons, so that the imperfect is used in these persons always to express exhortations. It is also used invariably in the 2nd person when the command is negative. The negative particle is then אַל.

The 1st person of the imperfect may express intention. This is called its voluntative use. It has then frequently a special ending ָ◌ה attached. This termination is also used when the 1st person has its cohortative signification (אֶקְטְלָה).

The 2nd and 3rd persons singular in some verbs have special forms when used jussively. In the קָטַל type of verb there is a distinction of form only in the Hiphil, where יַקְטֵל and תַּקְטֵל are the jussive forms of יַקְטִיל and תַּקְטִיל.

Translation Exercise.

Let us destroy that wicked city. May thy son be honoured in the eyes of the people. Do not conspire against the king. May thy name be great in the gate of thy people. Let us fight against our enemies. Do not destroy (sing.) the cities of our land.

---

§ 33. CONSECUTIVE TENSES.

The rule given for the use of the Hebrew tenses is regularly reversed when the conjunction "and" immediately precedes the Hebrew verb. Verbs introduced by the word "and" in narratives, if they denote complete action, are put in the imperfect tense; if they denote incomplete action, in the perfect (cf. § 27). This use of the tenses is called their consecutive use. A consecutive perfect is equivalent to an ordinary imperfect, and a consecutive imperfect to an ordinary perfect (see note *a*).

Consecutive imperfects sometimes have special forms. In the קָטַל type of verb יַקְטֵל is the form of the consecutive imperfect Hiphil.

The conjunction which introduces these tenses is known as "waw consecutive." Before imperfects it has a special consecutive form וַ, and the initial consonant of the imperfect is doubled after it (וַיִּקְטֹל). Before the first person singular, where the initial consonant is א, or when the preformative syllable is יְ (in Piels and Puals), this doubling cannot take place; in the former case the form of the conjunction is וָ.

NOTES.—(*a*) Of course, the meaning of the Hebrew tenses as understood by the Hebrews themselves was never reversed, it is rather our rendering of them that changes when they are consecutive. The nature of the idiom may be illustrated by such a sentence as: "I rose up and dressed and went out and took a walk and felt in consequence much refreshed." The Hebrew translation, after marking the actions as complete by the use of one perfect tense, proceeds to use imperfects which carry us back into the time when the actions were going on; as if we said: "I rose up and (then) I dress and go out and take a walk and feel much refreshed in consequence."

(*b*) It is important to observe that the consecutive usage of a tense is only permissible when the Hebrew conjunction immediately precedes the Hebrew verb. If any word intervenes, as in the sentence "Everything is thine, and from thy hand we have given to thee," it cannot be employed. As the Hebrew negative always precedes the verb which it negatives, it follows that the consecutive idiom is never employed in negative sentences.

(*c*) Beginners should never use a perfect after וְ to express complete action; וְקָטַל should always be understood in a consecutive sense. On the other hand, imperfects may be used after "simple *waw*" in a jussive sense; consecutive imperfects are always distinguished by the special form of the conjunction.

(*d*) The consecutive tenses are to some extent distinguished by a special accentuation (word-stress). In *perfects* (not in pause) the accent falls on the last syllable (except on נוּ, and in Hiphils וֹ or ־ָה or ־ִי). In *imperfects*, when the penultimate syllable is open, *i.e.* does not end in a consonant, the accent falls on it. The vowel of the final syllable shortens in consequence (*e.g.* וַיִּקָּטֶל). In verbs like קטל this change is only possible in the Niphal. It is unusual in the 1st person singular.

Translation Exercises.

(*a*) He became great and was honoured in the eyes of the people. He fought against the city and destroyed it. She wrote to him and sent her son. They disobeyed God's commandments and did not seek his ways. God heard their cry and visited them. Everything is thine and from thy hand we have given to thee. Do not conspire against us and we will not punish you.

(*b*) I will search for the book and will write to you. He will become great and be honoured. I will visit him and will swear as you have spoken to me. He consecrated the house to God and kept all his commandments. He stood beside the well and spoke to the people. I remembered the words of my father and did not speak. I will hear their cry and will visit them.

(*c*) He kept his commandments and hearkened to his words. We will keep his commandments and hearken to his words. She remembered his name and spoke to him. God visits his people and watches over them all the days of their lives. He will cut down the trees and will destroy all the houses. I will fight with his enemies and he will send his officers to me. He wrote many books and spoke many words.

§ 34. IMPERATIVES.

The forms are given in Table I. The second vowel of the imperative Ḳal (2nd sing. masc.) is *pathaḥ* or *ḥolem*, according to the stem-vowel of the imperfect. The imperative is not used in negative commands (see § 32). An English "that" clause after an imperative (or jussive) is translated into Hebrew by וְ followed by a second imperative (or jussive). "Sanctify yourselves that I may speak to you," is הִתְקַדְּשׁוּ וַאֲדַבְּרָה לָכֶם.

NOTE.—The 2nd sing. masc. may have a lengthened form in ָה, like the cohortative imperfect (קִטְלָה or קָטְלָה).

TRANSLATION EXERCISE.

Speak and I will hear. Write your names that I may send them. Visit us and we shall be honoured. Seek ye my ways. Pursue after them and fight against them. Do not punish (sing.) us. Divide this possession. Consecrate this day. Remember (sing.) my words and my commandments. Sacrifice (sing.) unto him sacrifices of righteousness.

---

§ 35. INFINITIVES.

Infinitives are not usually directly governed by other verbs: the preposition לְ is employed to introduce the infinitive (*e.g.* הָלַךְ לְלַמֵּד). After לְ the *sh'wa* of the infinitive Ḳal is silent; hence לִרְדֹּף.

NOTES.—(*a*) Pronominal suffixes are attached regularly to infinitives. The infinitive Ḳal then takes the form of a Segholate of the third class; the *sh'wa* following the middle radical is, however, vocal, unless the connective vowel of the suffix is vocal *sh'wa* (כָּתְבִי "my writing").

(*b*) The adverbial infinitives have a variety of uses. One of the most common is to emphasize a following perfect or imperfect; it may then be translated "certainly" or "surely."

(*c*) The ordinary infinitive Hithpael supplies the place of the adverbial infinitive of that form, and a similar usage prevails in the Piel. The adverbial infinitive Pual occurs only once in the Old Testament.

Translation Exercise.

I will not seek to pursue him. I went to speak to him. They learned to fight against their enemies. They went to seek him. I wrote to him to divide the people. Who is he to remember those things? They sought his life to destroy it. I will certainly remember. They will surely become great.

---

§ 36. PARTICIPLES.

These are adjectives, and are treated as such. They are used predicatively to express continuous actions. As nouns they denote the agent, in contrast to infinitives, which express actions. After the particle הִנֵּה ("behold") they generally have a future reference: "I am about to punish them"=הִנְנִי פֹּקֵד עֲלֵיהֶם. (For הִנֵּה with pronominal suffixes, see Table 13.)

Translation Exercise.

He found the prophet sitting under a tree. He is standing beside your son. He is riding upon an ass. The riders on horses have departed. Whom are you pursuing? And lo an angel was standing before him. I am seeking my father's asses. There is a time for seeking and a time for losing (letting perish). The conspirators swore to destroy the king's house. Behold I am about to destroy this wicked city.

---

§ 37. VERBAL IDIOMS.

Further examples of the special uses of the Piel, Niphal and Hiphil are given in vocabulary 37.

In the Hithpael of verbs initial sibilant, metathesis of the sibilant and the preceding dental ("point stop") regularly occurs; so הִתְשַׁמֵּר becomes הִשְׁתַּמֵּר. In such forms as הִצְטַדֵּק, Hithpael of צָדֵק, ת becomes ט under the influence of צ.

TRANSLATION EXERCISE.

Take heed lest ye be destroyed. I am about to set these officers in charge of the city. There is a time to justify and a time to condemn. They condemned the righteous man in place of justifying him. Who is righteous in God's eyes? Behold I will enter into judgment with thee (fem.), for thou hast bereaved many mothers. He sent her away from his house.

---

§ 38. NUMERALS.

Of the Hebrew numerals only אֶחָד, "one," is an adjective; the others are nouns, and may stand before or after the words they number. The units (2–10) are frequently put in the construct state.

Although the numerals 2–10 are nouns, they have each two forms, a masculine and a feminine. שְׁנַיִם "two," agrees with the noun it defines; in other cases the feminine is used with a masculine noun, and *vice versâ*.

Nouns defined by numerals are generally in the plural; but when the numeral is above ten, certain nouns (especially of weight and time) are put in the singular; so אִישׁ, יוֹם, שָׁנָה.

The masculine forms of the units should be learned first; the feminines and the tens are formed from these (see Table 15).

For "he is ten years of age," the Hebrew idiom is "he is a son of ten years."

TRANSLATION EXERCISE.

The man has 3 sons and 5 daughters. He is 6 years old. She is 20 years old (use בַּת). How many books are in the house? About 40. The old man has 2 sons and a daughter.

The horse is about 10 years old. He found 30 men there. He gave the 3 men bread and water. The city has 4 names. The king has 5 sons and 6 daughters.

---

§ 39. MISCELLANEOUS PRONOUNS.

Reflexive pronouns are not usually distinguished in Hebrew from the personal pronouns. But they are expressed by the reflexive forms of the verb, and נֶפֶשׁ with pronominal suffixes is often employed where we use a reflexive pronoun; so נַפְשׁוֹ = "himself."

One . . . another (reciprocal) is expressed by אִישׁ . . . רֵעֵהוּ or אִישׁ . . . אָחִיו. The indefinite pronouns are given in vocabulary 39. In sentences like "none went with him," the negative in Hebrew is joined to the verb; *e.g.* לֹא הָלַךְ אִישׁ אִתּוֹ. מִן־ "some," is, of course, the preposition "from" (cf. French *de*).

אֶחָד and אִישׁ are occasionally employed like the English indefinite article: אִישׁ נָבִיא "a prophet," or "a certain prophet."

Instead of the accusative forms of the personal pronouns given in § 6, verbal suffixes are largely employed. When attached to perfects, these suffixes are identical with the nominal suffixes of § 7 (cf. § 18), except that "me" is ־ַנִי, and "us" ־ָנוּ. When attached to imperfects or imperatives, the connective vowel is *ṣere* in place of *ḳameṣ*. ־ֵהוּ and ־ֶהָ are then usually employed for "him" and "her" respectively.

The principal changes which take place in the Ḳal forms when suffixes are attached are as follows:

1. In the perfect (*a*) *ḳameṣ* of the initial syllable becomes vocal *sh'wa*; (*b*) vocal *sh'wa* following the medial radical is replaced by *ḳameṣ* (and so also *pathaḥ* in the 3rd sing. masc. before light suffixes). Exx. קְטָלוּנִי, קְטָלָם.

2. In the perfect, 3rd sing. fem. retains its original ending, *i.e.*, takes the form קְטָלַת (or קְטָלָת before ־ָם, ־ָן and ־ָךְ), 2nd

sing. fem. retains the ending תִּי, and 2nd plur. masc. takes תוּ in place of תֶּם.

3. In imperfects in *pathaḥ* (and imperatives), *pathaḥ* or *sh'wa* following the medial radical is replaced by *kameṣ* when light suffixes are attached. Exx., יִשְׁמָעֵם, יִשְׁמָעוּם, יִשְׁמַעֲכֶם.

4. In imperfects in *ḥolem* ō becomes vocal *sh'wa*, except when the connective vowel of the suffix is vocal *sh'wa*, when ָ is substituted. Exx., יִקְטְלֵם, יִקְטָלְךָ.

5. Imperatives like קְטֹל take forms like קָטְלֵ (with *sh'wa* vocal) before suffixes.

Translation Exercise.

The officers spoke to one another. They departed each to his own house. Is there anything in the house? There is nothing. He gave me some of his bread. Why will ye destroy yourselves. He kept one and sent the other to his brother. They fastened them to one another. I have everything with me. They sanctified themselves.

PART II.

VERBS WHICH DIVERGE FROM THE ḲATAL TYPE.

---

§ 40. INTRODUCTORY.

Dissyllabic verbal stems, and they are the most numerous, are all inflected in fundamentally the same way. Still the presence of a guttural or *resh,* or of a weak consonant, produces certain variations from the *ḳatal* type. Some weak consonants (א, י, ו) are easily absorbed by a preceding vowel and lose their consonantal value; their quiescence then naturally involves changes in the vowels with which they coalesce. *Nun* shows its weakness in all languages by assimilating with an immediately following consonant. Gutturals have more affinity than other consonants for the sound *a,* which is therefore specially frequent before and after gutturals (*e.g.* as *pathaḥ* furtive); where other consonants are followed by simple *sh'wa* vocal they take the more distinct *ḥaṭephs,* and, further, they do not easily admit of being doubled.

Obviously the influence exercised by a guttural or by a weak consonant on verbal forms will depend upon its position as the first, second or third of the stem-consonants. Dissyllabic verbs, therefore, which diverge from the *ḳatal* type may be classified as initial guttural, medial guttural, final guttural, and so forth. It is, strictly speaking, an error to call such verbs irregular. They inflect according to definite rules, and as compared with the *ḳatal* type they often preserve older forms from which the others are departures. In particular, it may be noted that the preformative *ḥireḳ* of קטל is a deflection from an older *pathaḥ,* which explains and is even retained in many of the verbal forms which diverge from the *ḳatal* type.

In addition to the verbs already mentioned there is a class of monosyllabic stems, and another of partially monosyllabic stems.

It is simpler, and probably more accurate historically, to treat these verbs as originally monosyllables, and not as dissyllables which have become monosyllables. The beginner will find it well to learn the verbs with a guttural or a weak consonant in the stem by noting the divergencies from the *ḳatal* type. In the case of monosyllabic stems the comparison with קטל is not at all of the same help.

---

§ 41. VERBS INITIAL GUTTURAL.

Principal Features :—

(1) The form of vocal *sh'wa* after the initial guttural is generally ◌ֲ (א prefers ◌ֱ).

(2) The custom of not doubling a guttural is exemplified in the imperfect Niphal and its related parts. The preformative vowel is lengthened in compensation. (This rule applies also to verbs initial *resh.*)

(3) Where קטל has a performative *ḥireḳ*, these verbs either (*a*) retain the original *pathaḥ*, or (*b*) modify it only to *s'ghol.* (*a*) is usual in most imperfects Ḳal (יַחְכֹּל, יַעֲלֶה) ; (*b*) is found when the stem-vowel of the imperfect Ḳal is *pathaḥ*, and generally in other parts (יֶחְמַד).

(4) In the forms which have a preformative syllable there is a prevailing tendency for a *ḥaṭeph* corresponding to the preformative vowel to slip in after the initial guttural (יַחֲבֹשׁ, יֶחֱזַק). When the medial consonant is followed by a vocal *sh'wa* this *ḥaṭeph* becomes the corresponding short vowel (יַחַבְשׁוּ).

Supplementary Notes :—

(*a*) Regarding היה and חיה see page 50.

(*b*) The 2nd sing. fem. and 2nd plur. masc. imperative Ḳal take the forms of קטל, but sometimes *s'ghol* is found in place of *ḥireḳ*.

(*c*) Preformative *s·ghol* is replaced by *pathaḥ* when an accented termination is attached to the form, or when the accent shifts under the influence of *waw* consecutive (especially in perfect Hiphil). Elsewhere also *a* appears for *e*, or *e* for *a*.

(*d*) In the perfect Hiphil the vowels ◌ֱ ◌ֶ are sometimes replaced by ◌ֲ ◌ֵ, and in the Hophal ◌ֳ ◌ָ by ◌ֲ ◌ֹ.

(*e*) The preformative vowel of the adv. infin. Niphal is *pathaḥ.*

(*f*) Preformative *s·ghol* occurs in the Hiphils of other verbs than those of this class. Exx., הֶרְאָה, הֶלְאָה, הֶגְלָה.

---

§ 42. VERBS MEDIAL GUTTURAL.

Principal Features :—

(1) Vocal *sh·wa* following the medial radical is generally ◌ֲ.

(2) The refusal of gutturals (and *resh*) to be doubled is exemplified in the intensive forms. Before ר, and generally before א, the preceding vowels are lengthened in compensation (see Table 3).

(3) *Pathaḥ* appears in the imperative Ḳal where *ḥireḳ* is used in the *ḳatal* type (*e.g.* גַּאֲלִי but אֶהֱבִי). It is further preferred to *ṣere* (*a*) in the perfects Piel, especially of verbs medial ה or ח, (*b*) before the imperfect termination נָה of verbs medial ר. (Compare also note *b*.)

Supplementary Notes :—

*(*a*) Rule 1 does not apply to verbs medial *resh,* but in the intensive forms (where ר has not been doubled) it is followed by ◌ֲ in place of vocal *sh·wa* simple.

(*b*) There is a tendency for the stem-vowel of the imperfect Ḳal of these verbs, and of verbs medial *resh*, to become *pathaḥ.*

(*c*) The change of accent described in § 33 note *d* may be observed in the forms spoken of in rule 2 (*e.g.* וַיְבָרֶךְ).

(*d*) Verbs medial *aleph* need not be distinguished from this class, but א exercises a special influence in some forms (שְׁאֶלְתֶּם, שְׁאֶלְתִּיו). Compare rule 3.

---

§ 43. VERBS FINAL GUTTURAL.

Principal Features:—

(1) Where the vowel preceding the third radical of the *ḳatul* type is not *a*, these verbs introduce it before the guttural either as *pathaḥ* furtive or independently. (*a*) *Ḥolem* in the imperfect and imperative Ḳal, and *ṣere* except in participles and adv. infinitives, is replaced by *pathaḥ*; (*b*) *pathaḥ* furtive is employed in all other cases.

(2) Before תְּ of the 2nd sing. fem. perf. *pathaḥ* slips in to ease pronunciation (תְּ is not mutated and *sh'wa* is retained).

---

§ 44. VERBS INITIAL *ALEPH.*

Principal Features:—

(1) Vocal *sh'wa* following *aleph* is generally ֱ if not far from the accented syllable; but with לֶאֱכֹל and בֶּאֱכֹל compare בַּאֲכֹל and מֵאֲכֹל.

(2) *Aleph* shows a tendency to quiesce after the vowel of a preformative syllable. Quiescence occurs regularly in the imperfect Ḳal of five verbs (אָמַר, אָפָה, אָכַל, אָבָה, אָבַד),* and frequently in two other cases (אָחַז, אָסַף). The preformative vowel in these forms has become *ó* (< *â* < *a'*), as in יֹאמַר. The most common instance of quiescence elsewhere is לֵאמֹר (infin. of אָמַר).

(3) The preformative vowel of the imperfect Ḳal in other verbs than those already mentioned is *s'ghol* (יֶאֱהַב).

---

* Mnemonic: he *said*, (*take*, *gather*,) *bake* and *eat* if you *will* not *perish*.

(4) Where the preformative vowel of the imperfect Ḳal is ô the stem-vowel is *pathaḥ* (five verbs as above) or *ṣere* (יֹאחֵז and יֹסֵף). In pause (§ 7, note), the vowel is *ṣere* in every case except, generally, אָמַר (compare note *b*). אמר has a special consecutive form, וַיֹּאמֶר.

Supplementary Notes :—

*(*a*) Quiescent *aleph* may be omitted in writing, and is so always (1) after preformative *aleph, e.g.* אֹמַר, and (2) in יֹסֵף for יֹאסֵף (compare § 47, note *e*).

(*b*) A pausal imperfect, when at the same time consecutive, retains *pathaḥ* in the 2nd and 3rd persons singular.

(*c*) For the consecutive forms וַיֹּאחֶז and וַיֹּסֶף see § 33, note *d*.

(*d*) Pronominal suffixes are added to the form יֹאכֵל; hence יֹאכְלֵם, &c.

---

§ 45. VERBS FINAL *ALEPH*.

Principal Features :—

(1) When there is no termination attached to the stem, *aleph* quiesces and *pathaḥ* before it becomes *ḳameṣ*.

(2) Before consonantal terminations (not pronominal suffixes), *aleph* quiesces and the preceding vowel is generally *ṣere*; but before the ending נָה it is *s'ghol*, and in the perfect Ḳal *ḳameṣ* (generally).

(3) The preformative vowel of the Hophal is generally —.

Supplementary Notes :—

*(*a*) The mutation of the ת in perfect terminations shows that א has lost its consonantal value.

(*b*) Quiescent א may be omitted in writing.

(*c*) Forms due to the analogy of verbs final *yodh* are found occasionally in verbs of this class.

(*d*) Infinitives of a feminine form are preferred (לִקְרַאת, יִרְאָה).

(*e*) The final vowel of the consecutive imperfect Hiphil is specially often *ḥirek*.

(*f*) Participles feminine are frequently of the type מֹצֵאת.

(*g*) *Waw* consecutive has generally no effect on the accent of perfects (compare § 33 *d*).

---

§ 46. VERBS INITIAL *NUN*.

Principal Features:—

(1) When *nun* immediately precedes the medial radical it assimilates to it; *e.g.*, יִפֹּל from יִנְפֹּל.

(2) Most imperatives and infinitives of verbs imperfect in *pathaḥ* are formed directly from the imperfect, and so lose their initial *nun* (גַּשׁ from יִגַּשׁ; but נְפֹל). The lengthened imperative (גְּשָׁה), and a feminine segholate infinitive (גֶּשֶׁת), are then generally employed "in compensation."

(3) The preformative vowel of the Hophal is ֻ.

Supplementary Notes:—

*(*a*) Verbs medial guttural and pausal forms are usually exceptions to Rule 1 (but נִחַם, perfect Niphal).

*(*b*) When suffixes are attached to segholate infinitives the vowel of the monosyllable is *ḥirek*. For the form of the preposition in לָגֶשֶׁת see § 11, note.

*(*c*) For the special forms of נָתַן and נשׂא see Tables 7 and 14. The final נ of נתן assimilates before perfect terminations which commence with a consonant; so also in the infinitive.

*(*d*) The verb לקח ("to take") is treated in the same manner as verbs initial *nun*, except in the perfect Niphal (נִלְקַח). It is one of the verbs which retain old passive Ḳal forms; לֻקַּח (perfect) and יֻקַּח (imperfect) are more simply explained in this way than as Pual and Hophal respectively.

§ 47. VERBS INITIAL *YODH* AND *WAW*.

These two classes are combined in one, which exhibits the character of both. *Yodh* appears generally in the Ḳal and intensives, *waw* in the Niphal and causatives.

Principal Features :—

(1) In the imperfect Ḳal *yodh* coalesces with the (original) preformative *pathaḥ*, and the resultant vowel is *ê* or *î* (*ay* > *ê* > *î*). The final vowel of the first class is *ṣere* ; of the second, *pathaḥ*. Exx., יֵשֵׁב and יִירַשׁ.

(2) In the Niphal (perf. and partic.) and Hiphil the resultant vowel (from *aw*) is *ô* ; in the Hophal, generally וּ.

(3) The imperative and infinitive Ḳal, being usually formed directly from the imperfect, lose the initial consonant and have similar forms to those of the verbs initial *nun*.

(4) The imperfect Niphal follows the inflection of קטל, but the preformative vowel of the 1st sing. is *ḥireḳ*.

Supplementary Notes :—

*(*a*) Imperfects Ḳal of the type יֵשֵׁב occur in a small number of very common verbs ; in יֵדַע from יָדַע ("to know") *pathaḥ* is due to the guttural.

*(*b*) הָלַךְ is treated like a verb initial *yodh* (see Table 14). The infinitive with suffixes retains the vowel *s·ghol* (לֶכְתּוֹ).

*(*c*) *Yodh* and *waw* are not invariably restricted to the forms in which they usually occur. There are Hiphils which retain *yodh* (*e.g.* הֵיטִיב), and when the stem has a medial sibilant forms like הִצִּית occur. יוּכַל from יָכֹל ("be able"), is an imperfect Ḳal of a verb initial *waw*.

*(*d*) The Hophals of monosyllabic and partially monosyllabic stems are the same as in verbs of this class, and they may have influenced one another.

*(*e*) The omission of the quiescent stem consonant in writing makes it sometimes difficult to recognise certain forms. יְרְאוּ is

plural of יִירָא (compare יִרְאוּ from יִרְאֶה). יוֹסֵף from הוֹסִיף may be written יֹסֵף, which also stands for יֹאסֵף (§ 44).

(*f*) The rule given in § 33 note *d* applies to imperfects Ḳal of the type יֵשֵׁב, and to imperfects Hiphil (but always וַיֵּצֵא).

(*g*) For יָצָא see Table 12.

(*h*) Contracted forms such as וַיֵּדֶּה for וַיְיַדֶּה, are occasionally found in the Piẹl or Pual.

(*i*) Imperfects Hiphil like יֵיטִיב may be due simply to the Massorite scholars; they are difficult to explain phonetically.

---

§ 48. VERBS FINAL *YODH.*

Principal Features:—

(1) When no termination is attached to the stem, *yodh* coalesces with the preceding vowel, except in the passive participle Ḳal. The pre-Massorite representation of this final vowel was generally ה, and that is retained along with the Massorite vowel-sign. In perfects the vowel is ◌ָ, in imperfects and participles ◌ֶ, in imperatives ◌ֵ, (in adv. infinitives ◌ֹ or ◌ֵ).

(2) When a termination is attached to the stem, *yodh* either quiesces or is elided: (*a*) when the termination commences with a consonant quiescence takes place, and the resultant vowel in perfects is ◌ִי— (Ḳal and generally actives) or ◌ֵי—; before נָה it is ◌ֶי—; (*b*) if the termination is vocalic, *yodh* is elided (גָּלוּ from גָּלְיוּ); (*c*) in the 3rd sing. fem. *yodh* is elided and the termination is ◌ָת—, or most usually (a double feminine ending) ◌ְתָה— (hence גָּלָת and גָּלְתָה); (*d*) ordinary infinitives have a feminine ending וֹת in which the third radical is absorbed (גְּלוֹת).

(3) Jussive and consecutive imperfects have special shortened forms, got by dropping the ending ◌ֶה—. The full form is retained especially in the 1st person. In the Ḳal and Hiphil, when ◌ֶה— is dropped, a monosyllable is left, which generally becomes a dissyllable (like segholate nouns) by the insertion of a helping vowel. Shortened imperatives are also used.

Supplementary Notes :—

*(*a*) ת in perfect terminations necessarily mutates after the preceding vowel.

*(*b*) Examples of monosyllabic consecutive imperfects are וַיַּרְא (Kal and Hiphil; but וַתֵּרֶא), וַיֵּבְךְּ, וַיֵּט, וַיַּךְ, from רָאָה, בָּכָה, נָטָה, הִכָּה (נכה).

*(*c*) In Kal dissyllabic forms the preformative vowel either remains *ḥirek* (יִגֶל) or becomes *ṣere* (as in סֵפֶר); in the Hiphil it is regularly *s·ghol* (יֶגֶל as in מֶלֶךְ).

(*d*) The radical *yodh* is frequently found before the archaic plural ending וּן, in pause and in the feminine of participles (בֹּכִיָּה).

(*e*) Before pronominal suffixes the final vowels of the forms referred to in rule 1 are generally omitted; the stem of the 3rd sing. fem. perf. is formed like גָּלַת.

(*f*) Special cohortative forms (§ 32) of the imperfect are unusual.

(*g*) *Waw* consecutive generally does not affect the accent of perfects.

(*h*) Final *waw* rarely appears (הִשְׁתַּחֲוָה from שחו=שחה).

(*i*) Poetic and late forms of these verbs are often like those of verbs final *aleph*.

---

§ 49. VERBS היה AND חיה.

Principal Features :—

(1) *Sh·wa* vocal following the initial consonant is generally ֱ (but הֱיִי and חֲיִי).

(2) This *sh·wa* becomes silent when preceded by the conjunction וְ, or (in the case of infinitives) by the prepositions בְּ, כְּ, לְ, and מִ (*e.g.* לִהְיוֹת).

(3) In spite of the initial guttural the preformative vowel is generally *ḥirek*, as in קטל (but הֶחֱיָה). Similarly מִ before infinitives and וְ before perfects (but וֶהְיֵה and וֶחְיֵה).

(4) The special consecutive and jussive forms are יְהִי and יְחִי (pausal יֶהִי and יֶחִי).

§ 50. MONOSYLLABIC STEMS.

Principal Features :—

(1) The stem of these verbs, except in the intensives, is monosyllabic. The vowel of the stem varies according to the form, being generally similar to the characteristic stem-vowel of the *ḳatal* type.

(2) The preformative vowels, except in the imperfect Niphal, stand in an open syllable before the accent, and therefore are long: (*a*) generally *ḳameṣ*; (*b*) in Hiphil perfect and participle, *ṣere* (also in יֵבוֹשׁ); (*c*) in Hophal, וּ.

(3) In certain parts the stem becomes dissyllabic by the addition of an accented vowel, viz.: (*a*) וֹ before consonantal terminations in the perfects Niphal and Hiphil; (*b*) ֶי before נָה in the imperfect Ḳal (rarely Hiphil). In such cases the original stem-vowel of perfects changes (to וּ in the Niphal, to ֵ frequently in the Hiphil), and the preformative vowel becomes *sh'wâ* (before gutturals often *pathaḥ*); *e.g.* נְקוּמֹתִי.

(4) The intensive is generally formed either by doubling the final consonant (קוֹמֵם), or by doubling the whole stem (טִלְטֵל). Forms like קִיֵּם are unusual.

(5) The stem syllable generally retains the accent (even before the (verbal) endings וּ, ָה and ִי), but not in participles before nominal endings.

Supplementary Notes :—

*(*a*) The name form of these verbs is the infinitive; the vowel of the infinitive וּ, וֹ or ִי is also the vowel of the stem syllable of the imperfect. Imperfects in *û* and *î* have three forms (ordinary, jussive, and consecutive); *e.g.* יָקוּם, יָקֹם, יָּקָם; יָקִים, יָקֵם, יָּקֶם. In the 1st person the ordinary form is generally used for the consecutive also.

*(*b*) The vowel of the perfect Ḳal is generally *â*, but some verbs have *ô* (טוֹב, אוֹר, בּוֹשׁ), and מוּת has *ṣere*. The participle

has the same form as the perfect. There are also perfects in *î*, which are inflected like Hiphils; *e.g.* בִּין.

*(*c*) בּוֹא allows the analogy of verbs final *aleph* in some cases to prevail over the analogy of this class; *e.g.* הֵבֵאתָ generally for הֲבִיאֹתָ. N.B.—וַיָּבֵא and וַיָּבֹא.

(*d*) In the Niphal, the perfect and the participle are identical in form. Imperfect יִקּוֹם, if written יִלֹּם, appears like a verb initial *nun*.

(*e*) The perfects Hiphil and Hophal exhibit a type הִנִּיחַ as well as הֵנִיחַ (in this verb with distinctive meanings).

(*f*) The presence of *ṣere* as the stem-vowel of the Hiphil perfect depends largely on the accent; it is usual in the 2nd person plural, or with *waw* consecutive, or when pronominal suffixes are added.

(*g*) The lengthened imperative is accented on the termination before א, ה and ע (against rule 5).

---

§ 51. PARTIALLY MONOSYLLABIC STEMS.

Principal Features :—

(1) The stem of these verbs, except in intensives and in certain parts of the Ḳal (note *a*), is monosyllabic. The vowel of this monosyllable is generally *pathaḥ*. In the imperfect Ḳal and related parts it may be *ḥolem*, and in the Hiphil is generally *ṣere* (in the Niphal infinitive *ô* or *ê*).

(2) The preformative vowels are generally long and identical with those of the monosyllabic class, but they may be short with the initial stem-consonant doubled (note *b*).

(3) The final consonant is doubled when a termination is attached, and the stem-vowel is then shortened. Between the stem and consonantal endings an accented vowel is inserted (וֹ in perfects, ֶי in imperfects and imperatives). Preformative vowels in these forms become vocal *sh'was*, but *pathaḥ* before ה.

(4) The intensive forms are the same as those of last class.

(5) Before the terminations וּ, ָה— and ִי—, the accent generally remains on the stem.

Supplementary Notes :—

*(*a*) Dissyllabic stems (with the second radical repeated as a third) occur most frequently in transitive Ḳal perfects and in participles and adverbial infinitives Ḳal.

*(*b*) There are several types of imperfect Ḳal. The usual form in transitive verbs is like יָסֹב, in intransitive verbs like יֵקַל. Less usual forms are יִסֹּב and יִתַּם.

(*c*) The vowel of the monosyllable is not always that given in rule 1; *e.g.*, *pathaḥ* is usual in the 3rd plural perfect Hiphil when there is no guttural in the stem, and in other persons when there is (hence הֵסַבּוּ; but הֵרֵעוּ).

(*d*) When the monosyllabic stem ends in a guttural or *resh*, the stem-vowel is lengthened to compensate for the absence of doubling when terminations are attached; *e.g.* מָרָה from מַר (compare rule 3).

VOCABULARIES.

Vocabulary 1.

Father	אָב
Daughter	(f.) בַּת
Son	בֵּן
Earth, country	*(f.) אֶרֶץ
Book, letter	*סֵפֶר
Watchman	שֹׁמֵר
King	*מֶלֶךְ

Vocabulary 2.

Ass	חֲמוֹר
Well	(f.) בְּאֵר
Horse	סוּס
Lion	אֲרִי
Man, husband	אִישׁ
Send	שָׁלַח
Hear	שָׁמַע
Write	כָּתַב
Slay	הָרַג
Stand beside	עָמַד עַל־

Vocabulary 3.

People	עַם
Hill	הַר
Ox	פַּר
Not	לֹא
Upon, over	עַל־
In, among	בְּ
Like	כְּ
To	לְ

Vocabulary 4.

Good, beautiful	(f.) טוֹב, טוֹבָה
Bad, ugly ; worthless	(f.) רַע, רָעָה
Great (older); loud	(f.) גָּדוֹל, גְּדוֹלָה
Small (younger)	(f.) קָטוֹן, קְטַנָּה
High, tall	(f.) גָּבֹהַּ, גְּבֹהָה

Vocabulary 5.

Head	רֹאשׁ
Voice, sound	קוֹל
City	(f.) עִיר
Spirit	(f.) רוּחַ
Price	מְחִיר
Very	מְאֹד

Vocabulary 6.

Good	(pl. m.) טוֹבִים
Bad	„ רָעִים
Great	„ גְּדֹלִים
Small	„ קְטַנִּים
High	„ גְּבֹהִים

Vocabulary 8.

Watch, keep	שָׁמַר
Know	יָדַע
Give, place	נָתַן
I gave	נָתַתִּי
We gave	נָתַנּוּ

* The accented syllable in Hebrew is usually the last. Words marked by * are accented on the second last. See further, page vi.

Vocabulary 9.

Go, depart ... ... הָלַךְ
Go out ... ... יָצָא
There ... ... שָׁם
Thither ... ...* שָׁמָּה
Thence (from there) ... מִשָּׁם
Until (prep.) ... ... עַד
Morning ... ... בֹּקֶר

Vocabulary 11.

Why? ... ...לָמָּה, לָמָה *
Every, all ... ... כָּל־
Day ... ... יוֹם
To-day ... ... הַיּוֹם
Buy, acquire... ... ... קָנָה
For, at (a price) ... ... בְּ

Vocabulary 12.

Nose ... ... אַף
Mouth ... ... פֶּה
Heart... ... ... לֵב
Command ... ... מִצְוָה
Teaching, instruction, revelation ... ... תּוֹרָה
Wisdom ... ...חָכְמָה
Possession, property ... נַחֲלָה
Wall (of city) ... ... חוֹמָה
Obey (command) ... ... שָׁמַר

Vocabulary 13.

New ... ... חָדָשׁ
Wise ... ... חָכָם
Strong, mighty ... ... חָזָק

Vocabulary 14.

Hand ... ... (f.) יָד
Lip ... ... שָׂפָה
Word, thing ... ... דָּבָר
Prophet ... ... נָבִיא
Old, an elder ... ... זָקֵן
Holy ... ... קָדוֹשׁ
Righteous ... ... צַדִּיק
Shepherd ... ... רֹעֶה
Field, fields, country ... שָׂדֶה
Commands ... ... מִצְוֹת

Vocabulary 15.

Life ... ... חַיִּים
Old age ... ... זְקֻנִים
Youth ... ...נְעֻרִים
God ... ... אֱלֹהִים
Water ... ... מַיִם
Sky, heaven ... ... שָׁמַיִם
Mankind, men ... ... אָדָם

Vocabulary 16.

Before ... ... לִפְנֵי
After... ... ... אַחֲרֵי
Pursue ... ... (אַחֲרֵי) רָדַף
Army... ... ... צָבָא
Captain, officer ... ... שַׂר

Vocabulary 17.

Flesh ... ... בָּשָׂר
Grass ... ... חָצִיר
Judgment ... ...מִשְׁפָּט
Face, surface ... ... פָּנִים
Vengeance ... ... נְקָמָה

Vocabulary 20.

Master, lord	אָדוֹן, אֲדֹנִים
Unto, towards	אֶל־
Hearken to, obey	שָׁמַע אֶל־

Vocabulary 21.

Evening	עֶרֶב
Bread	לֶחֶם
Kindness	חֶסֶד
Foot	(f.) רֶגֶל
Way, road	דֶּרֶךְ
Ear	(f.) אֹזֶן
Holiness, sanctuary	קֹדֶשׁ
Queen	מַלְכָּה

Vocabulary 22.

Righteousness	(*i*) צֶדֶק
Knee	(*i*) בֶּרֶךְ
Opening	(*i*) פֶּתַח
Sacrifice	(*i*) זֶבַח
Gate	שַׁעַר
Youth	נַעַר
House	בַּיִת
Olive-tree	זַיִת
Eye	עַיִן
Death	מָוֶת
Kingdom	מַמְלָכָה
War, battle	מִלְחָמָה
Eternity	עוֹלָם
For ever	לְעוֹלָם

Vocabulary 23.

Judge	שֹׁפֵט
Priest	כֹּהֵן
Enemy	אֹיֵב
Mourning	מִסְפֵּד
Altar	(§ 14) מִזְבֵּחַ
Name	(§ 14) שֵׁם
Written	כָּתוּב
Nor	וְלֹא

Vocabulary 24.

Much, many	רַב
Bitter	מַר
Nose, anger	אַף
Mother	אֵם
Heart	(§ 14) לֵב
Arrow	חֵץ
Tree, wood	(1st declen.) עֵץ
Ordinance, decree	חֹק
Totality, whole	כֹּל

Vocabulary 25.

Father	אָב, אָבוֹת
Brother	אָח, אַחִים
Man	אִישׁ, אֲנָשִׁים
Woman	אִשָּׁה, נָשִׁים
Son	בֵּן, בָּנִים
Daughter	בַּת, בָּנוֹת
Day	יוֹם, יָמִים
City	עִיר, עָרִים
House	בַּיִת, בָּתִּים
Head	רֹאשׁ, רָאשִׁים
Mouth	פֶּה, פִּיּוֹת

Vocabulary 27.

Learn	לָמַד
Teach	לִמֵּד

Bind, conspire ... ... קָשַׁר
Look after, visit, inspect ... פָּקַד
Punish ... ... פָּקַד עַל־
Be consecrated ... ... קָדַשׁ
Consecrate, observe as holy קִדֵּשׁ
Grow up, become great ... גָּדַל
Be heavy ... ... כָּבֵד
Be honoured ... ... נִכְבַּד

Vocabulary 29.

Seek ... ... בִּקֵּשׁ
Speak ... ... דִּבֶּר
Swear ... ... נִשְׁבַּע
Fight ... ... נִלְחַם
Destroy ... ... הִשְׁמִיד
Divide ... ... הִבְדִּיל
By (agent) ... ... לְ
By (instrument) ... ... מִן־

Vocabulary 36.

Find, attain, come upon ... מָצָא
Ride ... ... רָכַב
Perish ... ... אָבַד
Let perish ... ... אִבֵּד
Time ... ...(f.) עֵת

Vocabulary 37.

Send away, see off, divorce שִׁלַּח
Take heed, beware ... ... נִשְׁמַר
Judge, do justice to ... שָׁפַט
Go to law with ... נִשְׁפַּט אֶת־
Be bereaved (of children) שָׁכֹל
Bereave ... ... שִׁכֵּל
Be righteous ... ... [צָדַק]
Justify, acquit, declare righteous ... ... הִצְדִּיק
Condemn ... ... הִרְשִׁיעַ
Set [one] in charge of הִפְקִיד[פ׳]עַל־

Vocabulary 38.

Year ... ... (§ 14) שָׁנָה
About (with numbers) ... כְּ

Vocabulary 39.

Anyone, someone ... אִישׁ, אִשָּׁה
Anything, something דָּבָר, כָּל־דָּבָר
Second, another ... ... שֵׁנִי
Few ... ... אֲחָדִים
Some ... ... מִן־
Whoever ... ... מִי
Whatever ... ... מָה
Each (one) ... ... אִישׁ, אִשָּׁה
Everyone ... ... כָּל־אִישׁ
Everything ... ... כָּל־דָּבָר
Life, soul ... ... (f.) נֶפֶשׁ
Friend, companion ... ... רֵעֶה
There is ... ... יֵשׁ
There is not ... ... אֵין
Become, there was ... ... הָיָה

TABLES

TABLE I. PARADIGM OF MODEL VERB.

		Kal.		*Niph'al.*
PERFECT	*Sing.* 3 *m.*	קָטַל	כָּבֵד	נִקְטַל
	f.	קָטְלָה	כָּבְדָה	נִקְטְלָה
	2 *m.*	קָטַלְתָּ	כָּבַדְתָּ	נִקְטַלְתָּ
	f.	קָטַלְתְּ	כָּבַדְתְּ	נִקְטַלְתְּ
	1 *c.*	קָטַלְתִּי	כָּבַדְתִּי	נִקְטַלְתִּי
	Plur. 3 *c.*	קָטְלוּ	כָּבְדוּ	נִקְטְלוּ
	2 *m.*	קְטַלְתֶּם	כְּבַדְתֶּם	נִקְטַלְתֶּם
	f.	קְטַלְתֶּן	כְּבַדְתֶּן	נִקְטַלְתֶּן
	1 *c.*	קָטַלְנוּ	כָּבַדְנוּ	נִקְטַלְנוּ
IMPERFECT	*Sing.* 3 *m.*	יִקְטֹל	יִכְבַּד	יִקָּטֵל
	2 *m.*	תִּקְטֹל	תִּכְבַּד	תִּקָּטֵל
	1 *c.*	אֶקְטֹל	אֶכְבַּד	אֶקָּטֵל
	Plur. 3 *m.*	יִקְטְלוּ	יִכְבְּדוּ	יִקָּטְלוּ
	2 *m.*	תִּקְטְלוּ	תִּכְבְּדוּ	תִּקָּטְלוּ
	1 *c.*	נִקְטֹל	נִכְבַּד	נִקָּטֵל
	Sing. 3 *f.*	תִּקְטֹל	תִּכְבַּד	תִּקָּטֵל
	2 *f.*	תִּקְטְלִי	תִּכְבְּדִי	תִּקָּטְלִי
	Plur. 3 *f.*	תִּקְטֹלְנָה	תִּכְבַּדְנָה	תִּקָּטַלְנָה
	2 *f.*	תִּקְטֹלְנָה	תִּכְבַּדְנָה	תִּקָּטַלְנָה
IMPERATIVE	*Sing.* 2 *m.*	קְטֹל	כְּבַד	הִקָּטֵל
	f.	קִטְלִי	כִּבְדִי	הִקָּטְלִי
	Plur. 2 *m.*	קִטְלוּ	כִּבְדוּ	הִקָּטְלוּ
	f.	קְטֹלְנָה	כְּבַדְנָה	הִקָּטַלְנָה
INFINITIVE	I. (*ordin.*)	קְטֹל	כְּבֹד	הִקָּטֵל
	II. (*adv.*)	קָטוֹל	כָּבוֹד	הִקָּטֹל, נִקְטֹל
PARTICIPLE	*act.*	קֹטֵל	כָּבֵד	
	pass.	קָטוּל		נִקְטָל

TABLE I. PARADIGM.—*cont.*

Pi'el.	*Pu'al.*	*Hithpa'el.*	*Hiph'il.*	*Hoph'al.*
קִטֵּל ,קִטַּל	קֻטַּל	הִתְקַטֵּל	הִקְטִיל	הָקְטַל
קִטְּלָה	קֻטְּלָה	הִתְקַטְּלָה	הִקְטִילָה	הָקְטְלָה
קִטַּלְתָּ	קֻטַּלְתָּ	הִתְקַטַּלְתָּ	הִקְטַלְתָּ	הָקְטַלְתָּ
קִטַּלְתְּ	קֻטַּלְתְּ	הִתְקַטַּלְתְּ	הִקְטַלְתְּ	הָקְטַלְתְּ
קִטַּלְתִּי	קֻטַּלְתִּי	הִתְקַטַּלְתִּי	הִקְטַלְתִּי	הָקְלַטְתִּי
קִטְּלוּ	קֻטְּלוּ	הִתְקַטְּלוּ	הִקְטִילוּ	הָקְטְלוּ
קִטַּלְתֶּם	קֻטַּלְתֶּם	הִתְקַטַּלְתֶּם	הִקְטַלְתֶּם	הָקְטַלְתֶּם
קִטַּלְתֶּן	קֻטַּלְתֶּן	הִתְקַטַּלְתֶּן	הִקְטַלְתֶּן	הָקְטַלְתֶּן
קִטַּלְנוּ	קֻטַּלְנוּ	הִתְקַטַּלְנוּ	הִקְטַלְנוּ	הָקְטַלְנוּ
יְקַטֵּל	יְקֻטַּל	יִתְקַטֵּל	יַקְטִיל	יָקְטַל
תְּקַטֵּל	תְּקֻטַּל	תִּתְקַטֵּל	תַּקְטִיל	תָּקְטַל
אֲקַטֵּל	אֲקֻטַּל	אֶתְקַטֵּל	אַקְטִיל	אָקְטַל
יְקַטְּלוּ	יְקֻטְּלוּ	יִתְקַטְּלוּ	יַקְטִילוּ	יָקְטְלוּ
תְּקַטְּלוּ	תְּקֻטְּלוּ	תִּתְקַטְּלוּ	תַּקְטִילוּ	תָּקְטְלוּ
נְקַטֵּל	נְקֻטַּל	נִתְקַטֵּל	נַקְטִיל	נָקְטַל
תְּקַטֵּל	תְּקֻטַּל	תִּתְקַטֵּל	תַּקְטִיל	תָּקְטַל
תְּקַטְּלִי	תְּקֻטְּלִי	תִּתְקַטְּלִי	תַּקְטִילִי	תָּקְטְלִי
תְּקַטֵּלְנָה	תְּקֻטַּלְנָה	תִּתְקַטֵּלְנָה	תַּקְטֵלְנָה	תָּקְטַלְנָה
תְּקַטֵּלְנָה	תְּקֻטַּלְנָה	תִּתְקַטֵּלְנָה	תַּקְטֵלְנָה	תָּקְטַלְנָה
קַטֵּל		הִתְקַטֵּל	הַקְטֵל	
קַטְּלִי		הִתְקַטְּלִי	הַקְטִילִי	
קַטְּלוּ		הִתְקַטְּלוּ	הַקְטִילוּ	
קַטֵּלְנָה		הִתְקַטֵּלְנָה	הַקְטֵלְנָה	
קַטֵּל	—	הִתְקַטֵּל	הַקְטִיל	—
קַטֹּל [קַטֵּל]	קֻטֹּל	[הִתְקַטֵּל]	הַקְטֵל	הָקְטֵל
מְקַטֵּל		מִתְקַטֵּל	מַקְטִיל	
	מְקֻטָּל			מָקְטָל

TABLE II. VERBS INITIAL GUTTURAL.

	Kal.		*Niph'al.*	*Hiph'il.*	*Hoph'al.*
PERF.	עָמַד	חָזַק	נֶעֱמַד	הֶעֱמִיד	הָעֳמַד
	עָמְדָה		נֶעֶמְדָה	הֶעֱמִידָה	הָעָמְדָה
	עָמַדְתָּ		נֶעֱמַדְתָּ	הֶעֱמַדְתָּ	הָעֳמַדְתָּ
	עָמַדְתְּ		נֶעֱמַדְתְּ	הֶעֱמַדְתְּ	הָעֳמַדְתְּ
	עָמַדְתִּי		נֶעֱמַדְתִּי	הֶעֱמַדְתִּי	הָעֳמַדְתִּי
	עָמְדוּ		נֶעֶמְדוּ	הֶעֱמִידוּ	הָעָמְדוּ
	עֲמַדְתֶּם		נֶעֱמַדְתֶּם	הֶעֱמַדְתֶּם	הָעֳמַדְתֶּם
	עֲמַדְתֶּן		נֶעֱמַדְתֶּן	הֶעֱמַדְתֶּן	הָעֳמַדְתֶּן
	עָמַדְנוּ		נֶעֱמַדְנוּ	הֶעֱמַדְנוּ	הָעֳמַדְנוּ
IMPERF.	יַעֲמֹד	יֶחֱזַק	יֵעָמֵד	יַעֲמִיד	יָעֳמַד
	תַּעֲמֹד	תֶּחֱזַק	תֵּעָמֵד	תַּעֲמִיד	תָּעֳמַד
	אֶעֱמֹד	אֶחֱזַק	אֵעָמֵד	אַעֲמִיד	אָעֳמַד
	יַעַמְדוּ	יֶחֶזְקוּ	יֵעָמְדוּ	יַעֲמִידוּ	יָעָמְדוּ
	תַּעַמְדוּ	תֶּחֶזְקוּ	תֵּעָמְדוּ	תַּעֲמִידוּ	תָּעָמְדוּ
	נַעֲמֹד	נֶחֱזַק	נֵעָמֵד	נַעֲמִיד	נָעֳמַד
	תַּעֲמֹד	תֶּחֱזַק	תֵּעָמֵד	תַּעֲמִיד	תָּעֳמַד
	תַּעַמְדִי	תֶּחֶזְקִי	תֵּעָמְדִי	תַּעֲמִידִי	תָּעָמְדִי
	תַּעֲמֹדְנָה	תֶּחֱזַקְנָה	תֵּעָמַדְנָה	תַּעֲמֵדְנָה	תָּעֳמַדְנָה
	תַּעֲמֹדְנָה	תֶּחֱזַקְנָה	תֵּעָמַדְנָה	תַּעֲמֵדְנָה	תָּעֳמַדְנָה
IMPERAT.	עֲמֹד	חֲזַק	הֵעָמֵד	הַעֲמֵד	
	עִמְדִי	חִזְקִי	הֵעָמְדִי	הַעֲמִידִי	
	עִמְדוּ	חִזְקוּ	הֵעָמְדוּ	הַעֲמִידוּ	
	עֲמֹדְנָה	חֲזַקְנָה	הֵעָמַדְנָה	הַעֲמֵדְנָה	
INFIN. I.	עֲמֹד		הֵעָמֵד	הַעֲמִיד	—
II.	עָמוֹד		הֵעָמוֹד, נַעֲמוֹד	הַעֲמֵד	הָעֳמֵד
PARTIC. *act.*	עֹמֵד			מַעֲמִיד	
pass.	עָמוּד		נֶעֱמָד		מָעֳמָד

TABLE III. MEDIAL GUTTURAL OR *RESH*.

	Ḳal.	*Niph'al.*	*Pi'el.*	*Pu'al.*	*Hithpa'el.*
PERF.	שָׁחַט	נִשְׁחַט	בֵּרַךְ	בֹּרַךְ	הִתְבָּרֵךְ
	שָׁחֲטָה	נִשְׁחֲטָה	בֵּרְכָה	בֹּרְכָה	הִתְבָּרְכָה
	שָׁחַטְתָּ	נִשְׁחַטְתָּ	בֵּרַכְתָּ	בֹּרַכְתָּ	הִתְבָּרַכְתָּ
	שָׁחַטְתְּ	נִשְׁחַטְתְּ	בֵּרַכְתְּ	בֹּרַכְתְּ	הִתְבָּרַכְתְּ
	שָׁחַטְתִּי	נִשְׁחַטְתִּי	בֵּרַכְתִּי	בֹּרַכְתִּי	הִתְבָּרַכְתִּי
	שָׁחֲטוּ	נִשְׁחֲטוּ	בֵּרְכוּ	בֹּרְכוּ	הִתְבָּרְכוּ
	שְׁחַטְתֶּם	נִשְׁחַטְתֶּם	בֵּרַכְתֶּם	בֹּרַכְתֶּם	הִתְבָּרַכְתֶּם
	שְׁחַטְתֶּן	נִשְׁחַטְתֶּן	בֵּרַכְתֶּן	בֹּרַכְתֶּן	הִתְבָּרַכְתֶּן
	שָׁחַטְנוּ	נִשְׁחַטְנוּ	בֵּרַכְנוּ	בֹּרַכְנוּ	הִתְבָּרַכְנוּ
IMPERF.	יִשְׁחַט	יִשָּׁחֵט	יְבָרֵךְ	יְבֹרַךְ	יִתְבָּרֵךְ
	תִּשְׁחַט	תִּשָּׁחֵט	תְּבָרֵךְ	תְּבֹרַךְ	תִּתְבָּרֵךְ
	אֶשְׁחַט	אֶשָּׁחֵט	אֲבָרֵךְ	אֲבֹרַךְ	אֶתְבָּרֵךְ
	יִשְׁחֲטוּ	יִשָּׁחֲטוּ	יְבָרְכוּ	יְבֹרְכוּ	יִתְבָּרְכוּ
	תִּשְׁחֲטוּ	תִּשָּׁחֲטוּ	תְּבָרְכוּ	תְּבֹרְכוּ	תִּתְבָּרְכוּ
	נִשְׁחַט	נִשָּׁחֵט	נְבָרֵךְ	נְבֹרַךְ	נִתְבָּרֵךְ
	תִּשְׁחַט	תִּשָּׁחֵט	תְּבָרֵךְ	תְּבֹרַךְ	תִּתְבָּרֵךְ
	תִּשְׁחֲטִי	תִּשָּׁחֲטִי	תְּבָרְכִי	תְּבֹרְכִי	תִּתְבָּרְכִי
	תִּשְׁחַטְנָה	תִּשָּׁחַטְנָה	תְּבָרַכְנָה	תְּבֹרַכְנָה	תִּתְבָּרַכְנָה
	תִּשְׁחַטְנָה	תִּשָּׁחַטְנָה	תְּבָרַכְנָה	תְּבֹרַכְנָה	תִּתְבָּרַכְנָה
IMPERAT.	שְׁחַט	הִשָּׁחֵט	בָּרֵךְ		הִתְבָּרֵךְ
	שַׁחֲטִי	הִשָּׁחֲטִי	בָּרְכִי		הִתְבָּרְכִי
	שַׁחֲטוּ	הִשָּׁחֲטוּ	בָּרְכוּ		הִתְבָּרְכוּ
	שְׁחַטְנָה	הִשָּׁחַטְנָה	בָּרֵכְנָה		הִתְבָּרַכְנָה
INFIN. I.	שְׁחֹט	הִשָּׁחֵט	בָּרֵךְ	—	הִתְבָּרֵךְ
II.	שָׁחוֹט	נִשְׁחוֹט	בָּרוֹךְ	—	—
PARTIC. *act.*	שֹׁחֵט	נִשְׁחָט	מְבָרֵךְ		מִתְבָּרֵךְ
pass.	שָׁחוּט			מְבֹרָךְ	

TABLE IV. VERBS FINAL GUTTURAL.

	Kal.	*Niph'al.*	*Pi'el.*	*Hithpa'el.*	*Hiph'il.*
Perf.	שָׁלַח	נִשְׁלַח	שִׁלַּח	הִשְׁתַּלַּח	הִשְׁלִיחַ
	שָׁלְחָה	נִשְׁלְחָה	שִׁלְּחָה	הִשְׁתַּלְּחָה	הִשְׁלִיחָה
	שָׁלַחְתָּ	נִשְׁלַחְתָּ	שִׁלַּחְתָּ	הִשְׁתַּלַּחְתָּ	הִשְׁלַחְתָּ
	שָׁלַחַתְּ	נִשְׁלַחַתְּ	שִׁלַּחַתְּ	הִשְׁתַּלַּחַתְּ	הִשְׁלַחַתְּ
	שָׁלַחְתִּי	נִשְׁלַחְתִּי	שִׁלַּחְתִּי	הִשְׁתַּלַּחְתִּי	הִשְׁלַחְתִּי
	שָׁלְחוּ	נִשְׁלְחוּ	שִׁלְּחוּ	הִשְׁתַּלְּחוּ	הִשְׁלִיחוּ
	שְׁלַחְתֶּם	נִשְׁלַחְתֶּם	שִׁלַּחְתֶּם	הִשְׁתַּלַּחְתֶּם	הִשְׁלַחְתֶּם
	שְׁלַחְתֶּן	נִשְׁלַחְתֶּן	שִׁלַּחְתֶּן	הִשְׁתַּלַּחְתֶּן	הִשְׁלַחְתֶּן
	שָׁלַחְנוּ	נִשְׁלַחְנוּ	שִׁלַּחְנוּ	הִשְׁתַּלַּחְנוּ	הִשְׁלַחְנוּ
Imperf.	יִשְׁלַח	יִשָּׁלַח	יְשַׁלַּח	יִשְׁתַּלַּח	יַשְׁלִיחַ
	תִּשְׁלַח	תִּשָּׁלַח	תְּשַׁלַּח	תִּשְׁתַּלַּח	תַּשְׁלִיחַ
	אֶשְׁלַח	אֶשָּׁלַח	אֲשַׁלַּח	אֶשְׁתַּלַּח	אַשְׁלִיחַ
	יִשְׁלְחוּ	יִשָּׁלְחוּ	יְשַׁלְּחוּ	יִשְׁתַּלְּחוּ	יַשְׁלִיחוּ
	תִּשְׁלְחוּ	תִּשָּׁלְחוּ	תְּשַׁלְּחוּ	תִּשְׁתַּלְּחוּ	תַּשְׁלִיחוּ
	נִשְׁלַח	נִשָּׁלַח	נְשַׁלַּח	נִשְׁתַּלַּח	נַשְׁלִיחַ
	תִּשְׁלַח	תִּשָּׁלַח	תְּשַׁלַּח	תִּשְׁתַּלַּח	תַּשְׁלִיחַ
	תִּשְׁלְחִי	תִּשָּׁלְחִי	תְּשַׁלְּחִי	תִּשְׁתַּלְּחִי	תַּשְׁלִיחִי
	תִּשְׁלַחְנָה	תִּשָּׁלַחְנָה	תְּשַׁלַּחְנָה	תִּשְׁתַּלַּחְנָה	תַּשְׁלַחְנָה
	תִּשְׁלַחְנָה	תִּשָּׁלַחְנָה	תְּשַׁלַּחְנָה	תִּשְׁתַּלַּחְנָה	תַּשְׁלַחְנָה
Imperat.	שְׁלַח	הִשָּׁלַח	שַׁלַּח	הִשְׁתַּלַּח	הַשְׁלַח
	שִׁלְחִי	הִשָּׁלְחִי	שַׁלְּחִי	הִשְׁתַּלְּחִי	הַשְׁלִיחִי
	שִׁלְחוּ	הִשָּׁלְחוּ	שַׁלְּחוּ	הִשְׁתַּלְּחוּ	הַשְׁלִיחוּ
	שְׁלַחְנָה	הִשָּׁלַחְנָה	שַׁלַּחְנָה	הִשְׁתַּלַּחְנָה	הַשְׁלַחְנָה
Infin. I.	שְׁלֹחַ	הִשָּׁלַח	שַׁלַּח	הִשְׁתַּלַּח	הַשְׁלִיחַ
II.	שָׁלוֹחַ	נִשְׁלֹחַ	[שַׁלֵּחַ]	[הִשְׁתַּלֵּחַ]	הַשְׁלֵחַ
Partic. *act.*	שֹׁלֵחַ		מְשַׁלֵּחַ	מִשְׁתַּלֵּחַ	מַשְׁלִיחַ
pass.	שָׁלוּחַ	נִשְׁלָח			

TABLE V. VERBS INITIAL *ALEPH*.

	Kal.		*Niph'al.*	*Hiph'il.*	*Hoph'al.*
PERF.	אָכַל אָכְלָה &c.	אָהֵב אָהֲבָה &c.	נֶאֱכַל נֶאֶכְלָה &c.	הֶאֱכִיל הֶאֱכִילָה &c.	הָאֳכַל הָאָכְלָה &c.
IMPERF.	יֹאכַל תֹּאכַל אֹכַל יֹאכְלוּ תֹּאכְלוּ נֹאכַל תֹּאכַל &c.	יֶאֱהַב תֶּאֱהַב אֶהַב יֶאֱהֲבוּ תֶּאֱהֲבוּ נֶאֱהַב תֶּאֱהַב &c.	יֵאָכֵל &c.	יַאֲכִיל &c.	יָאֳכַל &c.
IMPERAT.	אֱכֹל אִכְלִי אִכְלוּ אֱכֹלְנָה	אֱהַב אֶהֱבִי אֶהֱבוּ אֱהַבְנָה	הֵאָכֵל &c.	הַאֲכֵל &c.	—
INFIN. I.	אֱכֹל	אַהֲבָה (אֱהֹב)	הֵאָכֵל	הַאֲכִיל	—
II.	אָכוֹל	אָהֹב	הֵאָכֹל	הַאֲכֵל	הָאָכֵל
PARTIC. *act.*	אֹכֵל	אֹהֵב		מַאֲכִיל	
pass.	אָכוּל	אָהוּב	נֶאֱכָל		מָאֳכָל

TABLE VI. VERBS FINAL *ALEPH.*

	Kal.	*Niph'al.*	*Pi'el.*	*Hiph'il.*	*Hoph'al.*
PERF.	מָצָא	נִמְצָא	מִצֵּא	הִמְצִיא	הָמְצָא
	מָֽצְאָה	נִמְצְאָה	מִצְּאָה	הִמְצִיאָה	הָמְצְאָה
	מָצָאתָ	נִמְצֵאתָ	מִצֵּאתָ	הִמְצֵאתָ	&c.
	מָצָאת	נִמְצֵאת	מִצֵּאת	הִמְצֵאת	
	מָצָאתִי	נִמְצֵאתִי	מִצֵּאתִי	הִמְצֵאתִי	
	מָֽצְאוּ	נִמְצְאוּ	מִצְּאוּ	הִמְצִיאוּ	
	מְצָאתֶם	נִמְצֵאתֶם	מִצֵּאתֶם	הִמְצֵאתֶם	
	מְצָאתֶן	נִמְצֵאתֶן	מִצֵּאתֶן	הִמְצֵאתֶן	
	מָצָאנוּ	נִמְצֵאנוּ	מִצֵּאנוּ	הִמְצֵאנוּ	
IMPERF.	יִמְצָא	יִמָּצֵא	יְמַצֵּא	יַמְצִיא	יָמְצָא
	תִּמְצָא	תִּמָּצֵא	תְּמַצֵּא	תַּמְצִיא	תָּמְצָא
	אֶמְצָא	&c.	&c.	&c.	&c.
	יִמְצְאוּ				
	תִּמְצְאוּ				
	נִמְצָא				
	תִּמְצָא				
	תִּמְצְאִי				
	תִּמְצֶאנָה				
	תִּמְצֶאנָה				
IMPERAT.	מְצָא	הִמָּצֵא	מַצֵּא	הַמְצֵא	
	מִצְאִי	הִמָּצְאִי	מַצְּאִי	הַמְצִיאִי	
	מִצְאוּ	הִמָּצְאוּ	מַצְּאוּ	הַמְצִיאוּ	
	מְצֶאנָה	הִמָּצֶאנָה	מַצֶּאנָה	הַמְצֶאנָה	
INFIN. I.	מְצֹא	הִמָּצֵא	מַצֵּא	הַמְצִיא	
II.	מָצוֹא	נִמְצֹא	מַצֹּא [מַצֵּא]	הַמְצֵא	הָמְצֵא
PARTIC. *act.*	מֹצֵא		מְמַצֵּא	מַמְצִיא	מָמְצָא
pass.	מָצוּא	נִמְצָא			

TABLE VII. VERBS INITIAL *NUN.*

	Kal.		*Niph'al.*	*Hiph'il.*	*Hoph'al.*
PERF.	נָגַשׁ	נָתַן	נִגַּשׁ	הִגִּישׁ	הֻגַּשׁ
	נָגְשָׁה	נָתְנָה	נִגְּשָׁה	הִגִּישָׁה	הֻגְּשָׁה
	נָגַשְׁתָּ	נָתַתָּ	נִגַּשְׁתָּ	הִגַּשְׁתָּ	הֻגַּשְׁתָּ
	נָגַשְׁתְּ	נָתַתְּ	&c.	&c.	&c.
	נָגַשְׁתִּי	נָתַתִּי			
	נָגְשׁוּ	נָתְנוּ			
	נְגַשְׁתֶּם	נְתַתֶּם			
	נְגַשְׁתֶּן	נְתַתֶּן			
	נָגַשְׁנוּ	נָתַנּוּ			
IMPERF.	יִגַּשׁ	יִתֵּן	יִנָּגֵשׁ	יַגִּישׁ	יֻגַּשׁ
	תִּגַּשׁ	תִּתֵּן	תִּנָּגֵשׁ	תַּגִּישׁ	תֻּגַּשׁ
	אֶגַּשׁ	אֶתֵּן	&c.	&c.	&c.
	יִגְּשׁוּ	יִתְּנוּ			
	תִּגְּשׁוּ	תִּתְּנוּ			
	נִגַּשׁ	נִתֵּן			
	תִּגַּשׁ	תִּתֵּן			
	תִּגְּשִׁי	תִּתְּנִי			
	תִּגַּשְׁנָה	—			
	תִּגַּשְׁנָה	—			
IMPERAT.	גַּשׁ	תֵּן	הִנָּגֵשׁ	הַגֵּשׁ	
	גְּשִׁי	תְּנִי	הִנָּגְשִׁי	הַגִּישִׁי	
	גְּשׁוּ	תְּנוּ	הִנָּגְשׁוּ	הַגִּישׁוּ	
	גַּשְׁנָה	—	הִנָּגַשְׁנָה	הַגֵּשְׁנָה	
INFIN. I.	גֶּשֶׁת	תֵּת	הִנָּגֵשׁ	הַגִּישׁ	—
II.	נָגוֹשׁ	נָתוֹן	נִגֹּשׁ	הַגֵּשׁ	הֻגֵּשׁ
PARTIC. *act.*	נֹגֵשׁ	נֹתֵן		מַגִּישׁ	
pass.	נָגוּשׁ	נָתוּן	נִגָּשׁ		מֻגָּשׁ

TABLE VIII. VERBS INITIAL *YODH* AND *WAW*.

	Kal.		*Niph'al.*	*Hiph'il.*	*Hoph'al.*
PERF.	יָשַׁב	יָבֵשׁ	נוֹשַׁב	הוֹשִׁיב	הוּשַׁב
	יָשְׁבָה	יָבְשָׁה	נוֹשְׁבָה	הוֹשִׁיבָה	הוּשְׁבָה
	&c.	&c.	נוֹשַׁבְתָּ	הוֹשַׁבְתָּ	הוּשַׁבְתָּ
			נוֹשַׁבְתְּ	הוֹשַׁבְתְּ	הוּשַׁבְתְּ
			נוֹשַׁבְתִּי	הוֹשַׁבְתִּי	הוּשַׁבְתִּי
			נוֹשְׁבוּ	הוֹשִׁיבוּ	הוּשְׁבוּ
			נוֹשַׁבְתֶּם	הוֹשַׁבְתֶּם	הוּשַׁבְתֶּם
			נוֹשַׁבְתֶּן	הוֹשַׁבְתֶּן	הוּשַׁבְתֶּן
			נוֹשַׁבְנוּ	הוֹשַׁבְנוּ	הוּשַׁבְנוּ
IMPERF.	יֵשֵׁב	יִיבַשׁ	יִוָּשֵׁב	יוֹשִׁיב	יוּשַׁב
	תֵּשֵׁב	תִּיבַשׁ	תִּוָּשֵׁב	תּוֹשִׁיב	תּוּשַׁב
	אֵשֵׁב	אִיבַשׁ	אִוָּשֵׁב	אוֹשִׁיב	אוּשַׁב
	יֵשְׁבוּ	יִיבְשׁוּ	יִוָּשְׁבוּ	יוֹשִׁיבוּ	יוּשְׁבוּ
	תֵּשְׁבוּ	תִּיבְשׁוּ	תִּוָּשְׁבוּ	תּוֹשִׁיבוּ	תּוּשְׁבוּ
	נֵשֵׁב	נִיבַשׁ	נִוָּשֵׁב	נוֹשִׁיב	נוּשַׁב
	תֵּשֵׁב	תִּיבַשׁ	תִּוָּשֵׁב	תּוֹשִׁיב	תּוּשַׁב
	תֵּשְׁבִי	תִּיבְשִׁי	תִּוָּשְׁבִי	תּוֹשִׁיבִי	תּוּשְׁבִי
	תֵּשַׁבְנָה	תִּיבַשְׁנָה	תִּוָּשַׁבְנָה	תּוֹשֵׁבְנָה	תּוּשַׁבְנָה
	תֵּשַׁבְנָד	תִּיבַשְׁנָה	תִּוָּשַׁבְנָה	תּוֹשֵׁבְנָה	תּוּשַׁבְנָה
IMPERAT.	שֵׁב	—	הִוָּשֵׁב	הוֹשֵׁב	
	שְׁבִי	—	הִוָּשְׁבִי	הוֹשִׁיבִי	
	שְׁבוּ	—	הִוָּשְׁבוּ	הוֹשִׁיבוּ	
	שֵׁבְנָה	—	הִוָּשַׁבְנָה	הוֹשֵׁבְנָה	
INFIN. I.	שֶׁבֶת	יְבשׁ ,יְבשֶׁת	הִוָּשֵׁב	הוֹשִׁיב	—
II.	יָשׁוֹב	יָבשׁ	—	הוֹשֵׁב	—
PARTIC. *act.*	ישֵׁב	[יָבֵשׁ]		מוֹשִׁיב	
pass.	יָשׁוּב		נוֹשָׁב		מוּשָׁב

TABLE IX. VERBS FINAL *YODH* (*LAMEDH HE*).

	Ḳal.	*Niph'al.*	*Pi'el.*	*Pu'al.*	*Hiph'il.*
PERF.	גָּלָה	נִגְלָה	גִּלָּה	גֻּלָּה	הִגְלָה
	גָּלְתָה	נִגְלְתָה	גִּלְּתָה	גֻּלְּתָה	הִגְלְתָה
	גָּלִיתָ	נִגְלֵיתָ	גִּלִּיתָ	גֻּלֵּיתָ	הִגְלִיתָ
	גָּלִית	נִגְלֵית	גִּלִּית	גֻּלֵּית	הִגְלִית
	גָּלִיתִי	נִגְלֵיתִי	גִּלִּיתִי	גֻּלֵּיתִי	הִגְלִיתִי
	גָּלוּ	נִגְלוּ	גִּלּוּ	גֻּלּוּ	הִגְלִי
	גְּלִיתֶם	נִגְלֵיתֶם	גִּלִּיתֶם	גֻּלֵּיתֶם	הִגְלִיתֶם
	גְּלִיתֶן	נִגְלֵיתֶן	גִּלִּיתֶן	גֻּלֵּיתֶן	הִגְלִיתֶן
	גָּלִינוּ	נִגְלֵינוּ	גִּלִּינוּ	גֻּלֵּינוּ	הִגְלִינוּ
IMPERF.	יִגְלֶה	יִגָּלֶה	יְגַלֶּה	יְגֻלֶּה	יַגְלֶה
	תִּגְלֶה	תִּגָּלֶה	תְּגַלֶּה	תְּגֻלֶּה	תַּגְלֶה
	אֶגְלֶה	אֶגָּלֶה	אֲגַלֶּה	אֲגֻלֶּה	אַגְלֶה
	יִגְלוּ	יִגָּלוּ	יְגַלּוּ	יְגֻלּוּ	יַגְלוּ
	תִּגְלוּ	תִּגָּלוּ	תְּגַלּוּ	תְּגֻלּוּ	תַּגְלוּ
	נִגְלֶה	נִגָּלֶה	נְגַלֶּה	נְגֻלֶּה	נַגְלֶה
	תִּגְלֶה	תִּגָּלֶה	תְּגַלֶּה	תְּגֻלֶּה	תַּגְלֶה
	תִּגְלִי	תִּגָּלִי	תְּגַלִּי	תְּגֻלִּי	תַּגְלִי
	תִּגְלֶינָה	תִּגָּלֶינָה	תְּגַלֶּינָה	תְּגֻלֶּינָה	תַּגְלֶינָה
	תִּגְלֶינָה	תִּגָּלֶינָה	תְּגַלֶּינָה	תְּגֻלֶּינָה	תַּגְלֶינָה
IMPERAT.	גְּלֵה	הִגָּלֵה	גַּלֵּה		הַגְלֵה
	גְּלִי	הִגָּלִי	גַּלִּי		הַגְלִי
	גְּלוּ	הִגָּלוּ	גַּלּוּ		הַגְלוּ
	גְּלֶינָה	הִגָּלֶינָה	גַּלֶּינָה		הַגְלֶינָה
INFIN. I.	גְּלוֹת	הִגָּלוֹת	גַּלּוֹת	גֻּלּוֹת	הַגְלוֹת
II.	גָּלֹה	נִגְלֹה, [הִגָּלֵה]	גַּלֹּה, [גַּלֵּה]	—	הַגְלֵה
PARTIC. *act.*	גֹּלֶה		מְגַלֶּה		מַגְלֶה
pass.	גָּלוּי	נִגְלֶה		מְגֻלֶּה	

TABLE X. MONOSYLLABIC STEMS.

	Kal.	*Niph'al.*	*Polel.*	*Hiph'il.*	*Hoph'al.*
PERF.	קָם	נָקוֹם	קוֹמֵם	הֵקִים	הוּקַם
	קָמָה	נָקוֹמָה	קוֹמְמָה	הֵקִימָה	הוּקְמָה
	קַמְתָּ	נְקוּמוֹתָ	קוֹמַמְתָּ	הֲקִימוֹתָ	&c.
	קַמְתְּ	נְקוּמוֹת	קוֹמַמְתְּ	הֲקִימוֹת	
	קַמְתִּי	נְקוּמוֹתִי	קוֹמַמְתִּי	הֲקִימוֹתִי	
	קָמוּ	נָקוֹמוּ	קוֹמְמוּ	הֵקִימוּ	
	קַמְתֶּם	נְקוּמוֹתֶם	קוֹמַמְתֶּם	הֲקִימוֹתֶם	
	קַמְתֶּן	נְקוּמוֹתֶן	קוֹמַמְתֶּן	הֲקִימוֹתֶן	
	קַמְנוּ	נְקוּמוֹנוּ	קוֹמַמְנוּ	הֲקִימוֹנוּ	
IMPERF.	יָקוּם	יִקּוֹם	יְקוֹמֵם	יָקִים	יוּקַם
	תָּקוּם	תִּקּוֹם	תְּקוֹמֵם	תָּקִים	תּוּקַם
	אָקוּם	אֶקּוֹם	אֲקוֹמֵם	אָקִים	אוּקַם
	יָקוּמוּ	יִקּוֹמוּ	יְקוֹמְמוּ	יָקִימוּ	יוּקְמוּ
	תָּקוּמוּ	תִּקּוֹמוּ	תְּקוֹמְמוּ	תָּקִימוּ	תּוּקְמוּ
	נָקוּם	נִקּוֹם	נְקוֹמֵם	נָקִים	נוּקַם
	תָּקוּם	תִּקּוֹם	תְּקוֹמֵם	תָּקִים	תּוּקַם
	תָּקוּמִי	תִּקּוֹמִי	תְּקוֹמְמִי	תָּקִימִי	תּוּקְמִי
	תְּקוּמֶינָה	תִּקּוֹמְנָה	תְּקוֹמֵמְנָה	תָּקֵמְנָה	—
	תְּקוּמֶינָה	תִּקּוֹמְנָה	תְּקוֹמֵמְנָה	תָּקֵמְנָה	—
IMPERAT.	קוּם	הִקּוֹם	קוֹמֵם	הָקֵם	
	קוּמִי	הִקּוֹמִי	קוֹמְמִי	הָקִימִי	
	קוּמוּ	הִקּוֹמוּ	קוֹמְמוּ	הָקִימוּ	
	קֹמְנָה	הִקּוֹמְנָה	קוֹמֵמְנָה	הָקֵמְנָה	
INFIN. I.	קוּם	הִקּוֹם	קוֹמֵם	הָקִים	—
II.	קוֹם	הִקּוֹם, נָקוֹם	—	הָקֵם	—
PARTIC. *act.*	קָם		מְקוֹמֵם	מֵקִים	
pass.	קוּם	נָקוֹם			מוּקָם

TABLE XI. PARTIALLY MONOSYLLABIC STEMS.

	Kal.		*Niph'al.*	*Hiph'il.*	*Hoph'al.*
Perf.	סָבַב	קַל	נָסַב	הֵסֵב	הוּסַב
	סָבֲבָה	קַלָּה	נָסַבָּה	הֵסֵבָּה	הוּסַבָּה
	סַבּוֹתָ	קַלּוֹתָ	נְסַבּוֹתָ	הֲסִבּוֹתָ	הוּסַבּוֹתָ
	סַבּוֹת	קַלּוֹת	נְסַבּוֹת	הֲסִבּוֹת	&c.
	סַבּוֹתִי	קַלּוֹתִי	נְסַבּוֹתִי	הֲסִבּוֹתִי	
	סָבֲבוּ	קַלּוּ	נָסַבּוּ	הֵסַבּוּ	
	סַבּוֹתֶם	קַלּוֹתֶם	נְסַבּוֹתֶם	הֲסִבּוֹתֶם	
	סַבּוֹתֶן	קַלּוֹתֶן	נְסַבּוֹתֶן	הֲסִבּוֹתֶן	
	סַבּוֹנוּ	קַלּוֹנוּ	נְסַבּוֹנוּ	הֲסִבּוֹנוּ	
Imperf.	יָסֹב	יֵקַל	יִסַּב	יָסֵב	יוּסַב
	תָּסֹב	תֵּקַל	תִּסַּב	תָּסֵב	תּוּסַב
	אָסֹב	&c.	אֶסַּב	אָסֵב	אוּסַב
	יָסֹבּוּ		יִסַּבּוּ	יָסֵבּוּ	יוּסַבּוּ
	תָּסֹבּוּ		תִּסַּבּוּ	תָּסֵבּוּ	תּוּסַבּוּ
	נָסֹב		נִסַּב	נָסֵב	נוּסַב
	תָּסֹב		תִּסַּב	תָּסֵב	תּוּסַב
	תָּסֹבִּי		תִּסַּבִּי	תָּסֵבִּי	תּוּסַבִּי
	תְּסֻבֶּינָה		—	תְּסִבֶּינָה	—
	תְּסֻבֶּינָה		—	תְּסִבֶּינָה	—
Imperat.	סֹב	—	הִסַּב	הָסֵב	
	סֹבִּי (רָנִּי)	—	הִסַּבִּי	הָסֵבִּי	
	סֹבּוּ (רָנּוּ)	—	הִסַּבּוּ	הָסֵבּוּ	
	—	—	—	—	
Infin. I.	סֹב	—	הִסֵּב	הָסֵב	—
II.	סָבוֹב	—	הִסּוֹב	הָסֵב	—
Partic. *act.*	סֹבֵב	—		מֵסֵב	
pass.	סָבוּב	—	נָסָב		מוּסָב

TABLE XII.

INITIAL NUN:	נְשֹׁק:	יִשַּׁק	נָשַׁק	kiss
	שְׂאֵת (לָשֵׂאת):	יִשָּׂא	נָשָׂא	lift
	תֵּת:	יִתֵּן	נָתַן	give
INITIAL ALEPH:	אֱמֹר: וַיֹּאמֶר, לֵאמֹר:	יֹאמַר	אָמַר	say
FINAL ALEPH:	מְצֹא:	יִמְצָא	מָצָא	find
INITIAL YODH:	שֶׁבֶת (לָשֶׁבֶת)	יֵשֵׁב	יָשַׁב	sit, dwell
	צֵאת	יֵצֵא	יָצָא	go out
	הוֹסִיף: יָסַף:	יוֹסִיף	הוֹסִיף	add
	[Similarly לֶכֶת:	יֵלֵךְ	[הָלַךְ	go
*FINAL YODH (LAMED HE):	בְּכוֹת:	יִבְכֶּה	בָּכָה	weep
	רְאוֹת: וַיַּרְא, וַתֵּרֶא:	יִרְאֶה	רָאָה	see
	הֱיוֹת: וַיְהִי, לִהְיוֹת:	יִהְיֶה	הָיָה	become
MONOSYLLABIC STEMS:	קוּם:	יָקוּם	קָם	rise
	בּוֹא:	יָבוֹא	בָּא	come
	מוּת:	יָמוּת	מֵת	die
	לִין:	יָלִין	לָן	pass night

So also שׁוּב, return; גּוּר, sojourn.

N.B.—Consec. imperf. וַיָּקָם, וַיָּשָׁב, &c.; but וַיָּבֹא.

PARTIALLY MONOSYLLABIC STEMS:				
Hiph. perf. הֵרַע	[רֹעַ]:	יֵרַע	רַע	be bad
„ „ הֵמַר	[מֹר]:	יֵמַר	מַר	be bitter
INITIAL GUTTURAL:	עֲשׂוֹת:	יַעֲשֶׂה	עָשָׂה	do, make
	חֲדֹל:	יֶחְדַּל	חָדַל	cease
MEDIAL RESH:	בָּרֵךְ:	יְבָרֵךְ	בֵּרַךְ	bless

* See inflections of Perfect in Table IX.

TABLE XIII.

הִנֵּה or הֵן	מִן	כְּ or כְּמוֹ	עַל	אֶל
הִנְנִי	†מִמֶּנִּי	†כָּמוֹנִי	עָלַי	אֵלַי
הִנְּךָ	מִמְּךָ	כָּמוֹךָ	עָלֶיךָ	אֵלֶיךָ
הִנָּךְ	מִמֵּךְ	[כָּמוֹךְ]	עָלַיִךְ	אֵלַיִךְ
†הִנּוֹ (3), הִנֵּהוּ (1)	†מִמֶּנּוּ	כָּמוֹהוּ	עָלָיו	אֵלָיו
—	†מִמֶּנָּה	כָּמוֹהָ	עָלֶיהָ	אֵלֶיהָ
הִנְנוּ	†מִמֶּנּוּ	כָּמֹנוּ	עָלֵינוּ	אֵלֵינוּ
הִנְּכֶם	מִכֶּם	כָּכֶם	עֲלֵיכֶם	אֲלֵיכֶם
[הִנְּכֶן]	[מִכֶּן]	[כָּכֶן]	עֲלֵיכֶן	אֲלֵיכֶן
הִנָּם	מֵהֶם	כָּהֶם	עֲלֵיהֶם	אֲלֵיהֶם
[הִנָּן]	מֵהֶן	כָּהֵן	עֲלֵיהֶן	אֲלֵיהֶן

† usually הִנֵּה הוּא † ֶ accented. † וֹ accented throughout.

TABLE XIV.

פֶּה	אִשָּׁה	אָח	אָב
(*cons.* פִּי)	(*cons.* אֵשֶׁת)	(*cons.* אֲחִי)	(*cons.* אֲבִי)
פִּיךָ	אִשְׁתִּי	אָחִי	אָבִי
פִּיךְ	אִשְׁתְּךָ	אָחִיךָ	אָבִיךָ
פִּיו	&c.	&c.	אָבִיךְ
פִּיהָ	—	—	אָבִיו
פִּינוּ	בַּת	אַחִים	אָבִיהָ
&c.	בִּתִּי	אַחַי	אָבִינוּ
	בִּתְּךָ	אַחֶיךָ	אֲבִיכֶם
	&c.	אַחַיִךְ	&c.
		אֶחָיו	
		&c.	

TABLE XV. CARDINAL NUMBERS.

	Masc.	*Fem.*
1	אֶחָד	אַחַת
2	שְׁנַיִם	שְׁתַּיִם
3	שָׁלֹשׁ	שְׁלֹשָׁה
4	אַרְבַּע	אַרְבָּעָה
5	חָמֵשׁ	חֲמִשָּׁה
6	שֵׁשׁ	שִׁשָּׁה
7	שֶׁבַע	שִׁבְעָה
8	שְׁמֹנֶה	שְׁמֹנָה
9	תֵּשַׁע	תִּשְׁעָה
10	עֶשֶׂר	עֲשָׂרָה

20	עֶשְׂרִים	100	מֵאָה
30	שְׁלֹשִׁים	200	מָאתַיִם
40	אַרְבָּעִים	300	שְׁלֹשׁ מֵאוֹת
50	חֲמִשִּׁים		&c.
60	שִׁשִּׁים	1000	אֶלֶף
70	שִׁבְעִים	2000	אַלְפַּיִם
80	שְׁמֹנִים	3000	שְׁלֹשֶׁת אֲלָפִים
90	תִּשְׁעִים		&c.

www.ingramcontent.com/pod-product-compliance
Lightning Source LLC
LaVergne TN
LVHW020656100826
845148LV00012B/2519
* 9 7 8 1 6 0 6 0 8 1 0 1 3 *